O9-BUC-240

TWENTIETH CENTURY
INTERPRETATIONS

MAYNARD MACK, *Series Editor*
Yale University

NOW AVAILABLE
Collections of Critical Essays
ON

ALL FOR LOVE

THE FROGS

THE GREAT GATSBY

HAMLET

THE ICEMAN COMETH

JOB

SAMSON AGONISTES

THE SOUND AND THE FURY

TWELFTH NIGHT

WALDEN

TWENTIETH CENTURY INTERPRETATIONS
OF

HENRY V

TWENTIETH CENTURY INTERPRETATIONS OF
HENRY V

A Collection of Critical Essays

Edited by

RONALD BERMAN

Prentice-Hall, Inc. A SPECTRUM BOOK *Englewood Cliffs, N. J.*

 Library of Congress Catalog Card Number 68-14471. Printed in the United States of America.

Current printing (last number):
10 9 8 7 6 5 4 3

Contents

Introduction

by Ronald Berman

Biographical Sketch

The records of Shakespeare's life are so few that all we know of him may be set down in the briefest account. He was born in 1564 to Mary Arden and John Shakespeare. His father was a yeoman of Stratford who was important both in business and in public office. Scholars have rightly emphasized that the community he grew up in was "enlightened" [1] and that he received a substantial education. In 1582, at the age of eighteen, he married Anne Hathaway, several years his elder, and had a daughter, Suzanna, and twins, Hamnet and Judith, by 1585. He appears to have gone to London before the end of the decade.

Shakespeare's first plays (*1, 2, 3, Henry VI*) were performed during 1590-1592. They were successful enough to provoke a famous attack by Robert Greene in his *Groatsworth of Wit* (1592). His two long poems, *Venus and Adonis* and *The Rape of Lucrece,* dedicated to the Earl of Southampton, were published in 1593 and 1594. In 1594 he joined the Lord Chamberlain's company of actors. This gave him access to a strong organization, where his colleagues were some of the most talented performers and producers of the Elizabethan theater. Evidence of his mounting prosperity is probably to be seen in his purchase of New Place, Stratford, in 1597. The opening of the Globe Theatre in 1599 provided him with a new source of income and became the place of performance for most of his plays after that date. The great tragedies were acted there from roughly 1600-1608, and the romances from roughly 1608-1613.

The evidence for Shakespeare's high standing with his contempo-

[1] Peter Alexander, *Shakespeare's Life and Art* (New York, 1961), 20.

raries may be examined in E. K. Chambers' *William Shakespeare.*[2] He died in retirement at Stratford in 1616. The so-called First Folio, containing thirty-six of his plays in texts of varying reliability, was posthumously published by his friends John Heminge and Henry Condell in 1623.

Shakespeare's Histories and Tudor Politics

Shakespeare's longest sustained work is the group of plays we call the English histories. *Henry V,* the last of these, brings to a close the second tetralogy: the other plays in this sub-group are *Richard II* and both parts of *Henry IV.* All of these plays have some basis in cultural experience—from *Richard II,* which, with its emphasis on the problems of succession and usurpation, was recognized as affording a possible parable to the politics of the 1590s, to *Henry V,* which seriously examines the rights and limits of monarchy. In Shakespeare's lifetime the nature of history and the conduct of politics were subjects of the first importance. Men wrote endlessly about political relationships, from John Calvin down to the street-corner pamphleteers. We must not overlook the extent of this interest, for in every dimension of life it found expression: in the sermons of Lancelot Andrewes,[3] in the writings of Ralegh,[4] in the tracts of James I,[5] in the dedications of poems, in textbooks, and above all in the offerings of the theater. Here, for example, is Thomas Nashe's account of the reception of *Henry VI:* "How would it have ioyed braue *Talbot* (the terror of the French) to thinke that after he had lyne two hundred yeares in his Tombe, hee should triumphe againe on the Stage, and haue his bones newe embalmed with the teares of ten thousand spectators at least, (at seueral times) who, in the Tragedian that represents his person, imagine they behold him fresh bleeding?"[6]

There was a heavy component of political theory in intellectual life. The schoolboy would read about the politics of the classical world

[2] E. K. Chambers, *William Shakespeare,* II (Oxford, 1951), 186-237.

[3] Lancelot Andrewes, *Ninety-Six Sermons* (London, 1629).

[4] Sir Walter Ralegh, *The History of the World* (London, 1614).

[5] King James I, *The Political Works,* ed. C. H. McIlwain (Cambridge, Mass., 1918).

[6] *Pierce Penilesse,* quoted by Chambers, 188.

in Plutarch and, as he grew older, would be invited to translate this into contemporary terms. After the study of the classics, Milton wrote, "the next remove must be to the study of Politics; to know the beginning, end, and reasons of political societies." He proposes, quite literally, that education be concerned with the history of politics from Moses on to the development of Saxon common law.[7] The Tudor conduct books, such as Elyot's *The Governor,* give immensely detailed descriptions of the status and role of those who rule. Poetry itself, as in Ben Jonson's "To Penshurst," celebrated the governance of great families and indicated its sympathy for a world of hierarchical and intelligible relationships. This is to say nothing of the political tract, which, from Machiavelli's *Il Principe* to the polemics of John Knox against Mary Stuart, argued in a thousand ways for the proper distribution of power.

In short, the late Tudor and early Stuart monarchies were obsessed by history. They had good cause to be, for the sense of the past in the light of which they interpreted events both past and present was Augustinian. It viewed political life under the aspect of original sin, and, while it held out hope for peace and order, it was fully aware that human life never will attain to divine order.[8] The *Sermon of Obedience,* tenth of the famous *Homilies* of Elizabeth, gives us a clear picture of the possibilities of human history thus seen:

> Every degree of people, in their vocation, calling, and office, hath appointed to them their duty and order. Some are in high degree, some in low, some kings and princes, some inferiors and subjects, priests and laymen, masters and servants, fathers and children, husbands and wives, rich and poor, and every one hath need of other, so that all in all things is to be lauded and praised the goodly order of God, without the which, no house, no city, no common wealth, can continue and endure. For where there is no right order, there reigneth all abuse, carnal liberty, enormity, sin, and Babylonical confusion. Take away kings, princes, rulers, magistrates, judges, and such states of God's order, no man shall ride or go by the highway unrobbed, no man shall sleep in his own house or bed unkilled, no man shall keep his wife, children, and possessions in quietness, all things shall be common, and there must needs follow

[7] John Milton, "Of Education," *Milton's Prose,* ed. M. W. Wallace (Oxford, 1925), 153.

[8] See R. G. Collingwood, *The Idea of History* (Oxford, 1951), 57.

all mischief and utter destruction, both of souls, bodies, goods, and common wealths.[9]

The reign of Elizabeth was not the idyll that it is often made out to be by moderns. It was punctuated by rebellions and executions; it was for a generation beset by the Spanish Wars; from its beginning to its end it suffered a crisis of authority. Insofar as Shakespeare's histories reflect the world behind their composition, it is a world in which order is too dearly purchased—or simply not attainable at all. It is indisputably, however, a world of *political* experience.

Plot and Character

In plot *Henry V* is deceptive. The final cause of the play has occurred before the opening scene, and this cause is the deposition of Richard II, an event at a remove of many years. The rebellions of the *Henry IV* plays and of *Henry V* are a product of this deposition: they belong to a political movement more than a generation old. These events are not, however, purely political in the modern sense: they have a religious meaning which gives them their full dimension. As one historian has written, "when we consider Tudor 'political' thought we must look beyond the limits of what *we* regard as political, and reckon with much that we would now call 'religious' thought." [10] In Tudor theories of history, political acts are held to be acts of providence in that they reveal intention and consciousness in the workings of time. Hence the political chaos of these plays constitutes a form of retribution for the murder of a legitimate king. In this respect the plays follow Edward Hall's *The Union of the Two Noble and Illustre Families of Lancaster and York* (1548), which presents the deposition of Richard as a reenactment of man's original sin, and views subsequent English history as punishment for that guilt. This element of Hall's interpretation resembles the vision of human history after the Fall in *Paradise Lost.*

Character itself must be understood, in part, with reference to this providential scheme. Henry V is not entirely a "real" personality—

[9] Quoted in M. M. Reese, *The Cease of Majesty* (New York, 1961), 38. This is the best basic work on the background of the play.
[10] Felix Raab, *The English Face of Machiavelli* (London, 1964), 9.

he has elements in him of symbol. We are meant to take seriously the remark in the opening scene that "the King is full of grace and fair regard," [11] for this indicates that in Henry's person the Lancastrian line asserts a moral as well as political power. Here is Shakespeare's description of his character as a manifestation of Christian ideals:

> The breath no sooner left his father's body
> But that his wildness, mortified in him,
> Seem'd to die too. Yea, at that very moment
> Consideration like an angel came
> And whipp'd th' offending Adam out of him,
> Leaving his body as a paradise
> T' envelop and contain celestial spirits.
> (I, i, 25-31)

We cannot allow ourselves to view Henry as we would view the characters of novelistic realism. He is part of a historical but also of a religious environment. Indeed, the whole movement of Shakespeare's tetralogy—*Richard II, 1* and *2 Henry IV,* and *Henry V*—is toward the creation of a character who is indivisible from the role he must play. Toward the end of *2 Henry IV* the newly crowned king speaks of his own personality as a function of his new status:

> The tide of blood in me
> Hath proudly flow'd in vanity till now.
> Now doth it turn and ebb back to the sea,
> Where it shall mingle with the state of floods
> And flow henceforth in formal majesty.
> (V, ii, 129-133)

When Henry debates the invasion of France, when he considers the fate of his traitorous friends, when he argues with the soldiers on nightwatch, the motives of a flesh-and-blood man are modified by what he calls "right and conscience." One of the consistent features of *Henry V* is the debate between character as a complex of individual motives and character as an emblem or epitome of historical experience. We know, of course, how that debate is resolved. A good example may be found in the second scene of Act II: when Henry judges the traitors he states that he seeks no revenge as a man—but that they must

[11] All quotations are from the G. L. Kittredge edition of *The Complete Works* (New York, 1936).

die for conspiring against his "royal person." The character of the king has been formed between the anvil of historical guilt and the hammer of royal duty. Whatever action is a consequence of his debates with himself and his advisors is colored by this fact.

Images and Ideas

Within a play, as Francis Fergusson has shown in a fine essay on *Hamlet*,[12] the action may be following some specific form. In the case of *Hamlet* the main action—purging the realm of a moral disease—encompasses a series of smaller actions which define it by repeating it. In the case of *Henry V* there is also a dual structure. In one sense the action moves smoothly along the usual groove of motive-action-consequence; but in another sense the main action, which has to do with *choice*, is repeated in a succession of decisions between alternatives. The play is so set up that the choice between these alternatives introduces the ideas around which the play revolves: the rights of monarchy; its limits; the subordination of what is individual to what is historically necessary.

From the first scene these alternatives are stressed. When Henry opens the issue of the French war, he says to his advisors:

> We charge you in the name of God, take heed;
> For never two such kingdoms did contend
> Without much fall of blood, whose guiltless drops
> Are every one a woe, a sore complaint
> 'Gainst him whose wrong gives edge unto the swords
> That make such waste in brief mortality.
>
> (I, ii, 23-28)

Thus a hard line is drawn in *Henry V* between *la gloire* and something of a deeper and more legitimate nature. The powers of decision are conceived of in a poetry that tries intensely to give some sense of moral *difficulty*. The metaphors used by the king are "strong-lined" and attempt to convey the strain between the will and something which gives the will more justification than it can itself provide:

[12] Francis Fergusson, "The Meaning of Hamlet," *The Idea of a Theater* (Princeton, 1949).

We are no tyrant, but a Christian king,
Unto whose grace our passion is as subject
As are our wretches fett'red in our prisons.
(I, ii, 241-243)

For that I have laid by my majesty
And plodded like a man for working days.
(I, ii, 276-277)

Elsewhere we see the language striving to give the effect of moral difficulty and intensity. As indicated above, the king has "whipp'd" the offending Adam out of himself; reformation has come in an overpowering "flood"; his wildness has "mortified" in him. When he decides the fate of his former friends the alternatives are, characteristically, phrased in the language of struggle: "The mercy that was quick in us but late/By your own council is suppress'd and kill'd" (II, ii, 79-80).

In no other play is the name of God so omnipresent, and in no other play does the language intimate so directly the terrible distance between what is divine and what is human. It is as wrong to apologize for the motives of the king as it is to be above them—as wrong, in other words, to agree with Stoll as with Van Doren.[13] The inner structure permits us to visualize continually the play of moral opposites. When the French king asks "what follows?" from the choice Henry has allowed him, we go from a vision of peace and legitimacy to one of quite another kind:

Bloody constraint; for if you hide the crown
Even in your hearts, there will he rake for it.
Therefore in fiery tempest is he coming,
In thunder and in earthquake, like a Jove;
That, if requiring fail, he will compel;
And bids you, in the bowels of the Lord,
Deliver up the crown, and to take mercy
On the poor souls for whom this hungry war
Opens his vasty jaws; and on your head
Turns he the widows' tears, the orphans' cries,
The dead men's blood, the pining maidens' groans,

[13] See the excerpts from Elmer Edgar Stoll and Mark Van Doren below.

> For husbands, fathers, and betrothed lovers
> That shall be swallowed in this controversy.
> (II, iv, 97-109)

Miss Spurgeon has written of the dominant imagery of flight in this play, a kind of imagery which gives poetic sanction to the soaring spirit of its protagonist.[14] But this passage, self-evidently, reveals another kind of imagery, which is reiterated in every act. It is imagery which dwells on the destruction of families, the slaughter of the innocent, the extinction of inheritance. It is permeated by the idea that there are alternatives for the human will itself: between the form of order and those other anarchic forms of which the Elizabethans were fully as aware as ourselves.

The duality of this kind of language is itself a theme: as Felix Raab has put it, "in Tudor historiography generally, the tension between human will and divine prescription is painfully evident."[15] The crucial events of the play invariably involve some tragic choice. They hang on alternatives of the kind stated before the gates of Harfleur,

> Whiles yet the cool and temperate wind of grace
> O'erblows the filthy and contagious clouds.
> (III, iii, 30-31)

There is nothing sanctified about the English army, and nothing in the nature of its leader which can prevent order from turning into anarchy. They are men, like any other, and they will rape and loot no differently from the armies of the twentieth century. The essential honesty of the play, its hostile critics to the contrary, is that this duality is acknowledged. Henry tells his men to "disguise fair nature" and take on that "terrible aspect" which is, after all, the other face of humanity. It is especially clear to the cool-headed Constable of France that the demonic is but another aspect of the rational. "How terrible in constant resolution" Henry is, he says to the sublimely unenlightened Dauphin.

In human affairs, the gulf between vision and action forces us to be aware of their duality. So too in Shakespeare's play. The state of man is first likened to the bees, who,

[14] See the excerpt from Caroline F. E. Spurgeon below.
[15] Raab, 69.

> like soldiers armed in their stings
> Make boot upon the summer's velvet buds,
> Which pillage they with merry march bring home
> To the tent-royal of their emperor,
> Who, busied in his majesty, surveys
> The singing masons building roofs of gold.
> (I, ii, 193-198)

But action displaces vision, and the parable takes historical form in terms of rape and murder, arson and looting. There is a great distance between the roofs of gold and the dunghills of the camp, where the smell of human bodies "shall breed a plague in France." The integrity of the play consists in its refusal to forget realities, in its insistence on unfolding the thousand small tragedies which give to ideology a larger and more ironical framework. One thinks not only of the condition of the English army, of the deaths of York and Suffolk, of the brutal fate of the boys of the camp, but also of the refrain which says, "O, be sick, great greatness,/And bid thy ceremony give thee cure!" (IV, i, 268-269).

Theme

As we can see from the essays in this volume, the theme of *Henry V* has been variously identified. If we are to side with Van Doren we shall find the theme of the play to be merely that of *la gloire*. Other choices run from *machtpolitik* to burlesque, demanding that we see the central figure as either a Bismarck or a Chaplinesque Great Dictator. My own conception of the theme is that it has to do with Humanism itself. *Henry V* seems to illustrate the central historical issue of the Renaissance—the problem of putting ideas and ideals into action.

This is a central theme of Thucydides, Herodotus, and Homer, as well as of Plutarch—all writers whom the Renaissance educated knew and admired. Their heroes are Themistocles, Pericles, Darius, Odysseus, men of bold outline who create their own private and public destinies. They exempt themselves from the conditions of general historical experience, and they are set apart from their world by the quality of their minds and the effect of their acts. Perhaps most important, they embody ideals of *virtu* central to their cultures. In C. M. Bowra's words, "a man served the state best by being himself in the full range of his nobility." [16] His selfhood, in other terms, was part of his civilization, and was admirable to the extent that it served the *polis*. Classical admiration for the exemplary hero was deeply rooted in the Renaissance.

It was not simply the military nor even the chivalric ideals which were celebrated: Marvell's Cromwell, Henry King's Gustavus Adolphus, and especially Donne's Prince Henry are also versions of what Plato and Zeno termed divine ideas in action. Prince Henry was apotheosized by Donne because he could break the yoke of Necessity, and impose on the material world a vision that came directly from the world beyond Nature. Was he not his

> . . . great fathers greatest instrument,
> And activ'st spirit, to convey and tie
> This soule of peace, through Christianity?
> Was it not well beleev'd, that hee would make
> This generall peace, th' Eternall overtake . . .[17]

The statement is typological; Prince Henry is a form of the Holy Spirit itself. Later, in the poetry of Henry King,[18] Gustavus Adolphus becomes a form not only of Platonic perfection but also of perfected Protestantism. In Marvell, Cromwell becomes a form of Providence—or, as J. A. Mazzeo has suggested, the incarnation of Davidic kingship.[19] Shakespeare's prince, like these other humanistic heroes, is conceived of as beyond the limitations of nature, able to impose the order of philosophy on the protean world of history. We may sense a contradiction between ideas of the fated nature of history and the ability to change it; between the Christian concept of character and the heroic capacity of mind. But that is a contradiction with which the Elizabethans were able to coexist.

[16] C. M. Bowra, *The Greek Experience* (New York, 1957), 32.

[17] John Donne, "Elegie upon the untimely death of the incomparable Prince Henry," *The Poems of John Donne,* ed. H. J. Grierson (Oxford, 1912), 268.

[18] See Ronald Berman, *Henry King and the Seventeenth Century* (London, 1964), 115-16.

[19] J. A. Mazzeo, *Renaissance and Seventeenth-Century Studies* (New York, 1964), 183-208. Mazzeo summarizes the nature of "figural interpretation" and the course of recent research into it.

From the first, Henry V is invested with Platonic majesty. Canterbury praises him for his miraculous reformation, and then adds, using an especially significant image, that Henry's intellect is pragmatic in an important way:

> Turn him to any cause of policy,
> The Gordian knot of it he will unloose.
> (I, i, 45-46)

We feel through the image the force of an empirical mind, the mastery of what would be inextricable by the ordinary power of the will. The king is from the outset marked by an ability to know the real from the rhetorical. Canterbury presses the idea that Henry has become a "sudden scholar," and then pursues his train of thought with more precision. He shows that a particular kind of knowledge is involved, stating that Henry is a master of three pre-eminent disciplines: "hear him but reason in divinity," he says, and "you would desire the King were made a prelate." Beneath the exaggeration (which anticipates the praise so eagerly sought by James I and so willingly granted by his court) is a reasonable conception. Henry knows the science which contains the cosmological and religious rationale for authority, and which supplies the hieratic framework of its application. The ability to "debate of commonwealth affairs" speaks for itself; it is a link with heroes like Themistocles and Pericles. His ability to "discourse of war" implies mastery of the fundamental kingly art. Most important of all, however, is the principle which unifies all his kinds of knowledge. The archbishop acknowledges that

> . . . the art and practic part of life
> Must be the mistress to this theoric.
> (I, i, 51-52)

Henry then, is primarily a solver of problems, and we are convinced of this by his handling of "theoric" throughout the first act. The involved reasoning about succession and the Salic law points neither to Shakespeare's fondness for extraneous rhetoric nor to Henry's aptitude for sophism. It is a mark of the practical mind, which seeks to convert ideas into action.

Henry V is a hero of moderation rather than of magnificence. J. H. Walter goes so far as to suggest that the conversion of the prince follows the writings of Bernard of Clairvaux, who urged reformation through "consideration"—or what was later called meditation.[20] It is this which inspires his policy, and which gives it a higher sanction. Medieval and Tudor historians, Walter writes, "saw in the events they described the unfolding of God's plan, history for them was still a handmaid to theology. . . . Henry V, the epic hero and the agent of God's plan, must therefore be divinely inspired and dedicated: he is every bit as dedicated as is 'pius Aeneas' to follow the divine plan." Henry's will to power then is not like Tamburlaine's crude drive for aggrandizement.[21] Nor is he chivalric in any empty romantic sense. He is essentially the model of a humanist prince.

It is important to recognize how this conception of the king is worked out in terms of plot and language. The lengthy discussion of Salic law was of much greater interest to its first audience than we may suppose. It shows a king dealing at firsthand with a "cause of policy" and unwinding it. What is most noticeable in this scene is Henry's moderation, and the language of faith in which it is expressed. Like the ideal prince in Erasmus' tractate on the education of the good ruler, he brings to bear on the matter of politics the more inclusive framework of religion. When he says, "May I with right and conscience make this claim?" we are intended to see that he is in fact subordinate to these great demands. The episodes of the French ambassadors and the treason of Grey, Scroop, and Cambridge also indicate the moral allegiances of the king. In neither case does Henry act from personal motives. In the first situation Shakespeare takes pains to show the king's "rightful hand in a well-hallow'd cause." In the second, the dialogue of justice and mercy—familiar not only in *The Merchant of Venice* but in cultural life as a whole—is resolved, correctly, in favor of the former. There is, after all, a very close correspondence here to the situation of Elizabeth, who disseminated Homily 33 in 1571:

> He that nameth rebellion nameth not a singular or one only sin, as is theft, robbery, murder and such like, but he nameth the whole puddle and sink of all sins against God and man, against his prince, his country, his parents, his children, his kinsfolk, his friends, and against all men

[20] *Henry V,* ed. J. H. Walter (London, 1954), xxii.

[21] See an argument to the contrary in Irving Ribner's *The English History Play in the Age of Shakespeare* (Princeton, 1957), 183.

> universally; all sins, I say, against God and all men heaped together, nameth he that nameth rebellion.[22]

We may not like the tone of the homily, and we may be put off by the resolution of the affair in terms of justice rather than mercy, but we ought to recognize that Henry is making the only possible choice. This is the way in which the mind of humanism disposes its political ideas.

On the other hand, the dialogue of justice and mercy may have another resolution. When the soldier Williams is judged for his offense of lese-majesty there is a dialogue among Fluellen, who urges death, the King, who grants mercy, and the soldier himself, who delivers the reason for a proper judgment:

> *Flu.* An please your Majesty, let his neck answer for it, if there is any martial law in the world.
>
> *King.* How canst thou make me satisfaction?
>
> *Will.* All offences, my lord, come from the heart. Never came any from mine that might offend your Majesty.
>
> (IV, viii, 45-51)

In this case the matter turns out "right" for the modern audience, but only because the king, in his role of humanist interlocutor, has satisfied himself of the legitimacy of the argument. Throughout *Henry V* what Hamlet called "the conscience of the king" operates as the reminder of a higher order of justice. It makes certain that decisions are undertaken with the arbitration of ideas that are more than personal and indeed more than secular. Surely nothing is more central to humanism than this concern.

The Audience Then and Now

We can only guess at the effect of *Henry V* upon its immediate audience. The lead was played by Richard Burbage, and it would seem that granted the subject, the nature of the play, and its casting, it must have been a success. Writing of a pre-Shakespearean Henry V play, Thomas Nashe had rejoiced in "what a glorious thing it is to have *Henrie* the Fifth represented on the stage, leading the French

[22] Quoted in Reese, 40.

king prisoner. . . ." [23] The extensive argument of Dover Wilson on the appropriateness of the play to the times ought to be considered; [24] the last year of the century was full of preparations for war and witnessed to some extent the renewal of the spirit of both Agincourt and the Armada. Not until the eighteenth century, however, do we find *Henry V* being performed with any regularity. It was in the nature of things overshadowed by the greater plays of the author—and, as Dr. Johnson shrewdly noted, it suffered by the general decline of interest in medieval history. The great subject of the seventeenth century was the Civil War, and it may be supposed that with the end of the medieval synthesis such a work as this was bound to be discarded. It was replaced by Restoration heroic tragedy, which was more operatic, blatant, and expressive of the reigning modes of thought and sensibility.

The play's value for the present is much easier to estimate, for rarely has a play of this kind stirred so much ideological controversy. The essays that follow are in effect a commentary on this; critics have divided themselves into liberals and conservatives. Some, like Dr. Johnson, have admired the play's conception and accepted the values upon which it is based. Others, like Hazlitt, viewed it as a satire on the *ancien régime,* and applauded anything in it which seemed to undercut hierarchy, feudalism, and Christian politics. The Johnsonians have found their voice in Dover Wilson's *The Fortunes of Falstaff,* which justifies the play and the beliefs upon which it rests. Those who follow Hazlitt have found their voice in Van Doren, who views the play as an essentially trivial representation of mere military aggression. Of the two, I find Dover Wilson more convincing. It is, I think, quite clear that Shakespeare does not glorify war; he only comprehends it. It is equally clear that his very considerable accomplishment has been to unify the matter of epic and history; to make the former more credible and the latter more human than any of the sources available to him.

[23] From *Pierce Penilesse,* quoted by Eugene Waith, *Shakespeare: The Histories* (Englewood Cliffs, 1965), 1.

[24] *Henry V,* ed. J. Dover Wilson (Cambridge, 1947), vii-xv.

PART ONE

Background

The Victorious Acts of King Henry V

by Lily B. Campbell

The Arden editor of Shakespeare's *Life of King Henry the Fifth,* H. A. Evans, sums up the common view of the play when he says that "its interest is epic rather than dramatic; it is the nearest approach on the part of the author to a national epic."[1] The historical mirrors that Shakespeare held up to England before he wrote of Henry V were mirrors in which the Elizabethans could see their own national problems being acted out on the stage before them, and in which they could witness the eternal justice of God in the affairs of the body politic. They showed the conflicts of the age which endangered the state, threatening its peace and security. But in *Henry V* the English are mirrored triumphant in a righteous cause, achieving victory through the blessing of God. A mood of exultation pervades the play. Henry V stands as the ideal hero in contrast with the troubled John, the deposed Richard, the rebel Henry IV; for the traditional conception of Henry V was of a hero-king, and about his dominant figure Shakespeare chose to fashion a hero-play. The theme of the play is war, and the progress of the warrior-hero is the progress of the play. Thus the play becomes in form and content epic.

This traditional view of Henry V as the hero-king of England, Kingsford traces to the official biography by Tito Livio, written by that Italian historian at the suggestion of his English patron, Humphrey Duke of Gloucester, brother of Henry V and protector during

"The Victorious Acts of King Henry V," by Lily B. Campbell. From Shakespeare's 'Histories': Mirrors of Elizabethan Policy *(San Marino, Huntington Library, 1947).*

[1] (London, 1917), p. xli.

the minority of Henry VI.[2] Tito Livio dedicated his work to the young king, offering it as a guide by which he might follow in his father's footsteps. Yet since it was, perforce, an account of Henry V's wars that he had written, he felt called upon to explain:

> Not that I preferr and laude warr and discention, rather than tranquillitie and peace; but if thou maiest have none honest peace, that then thou shalt seeke peace and rest with victorie to both thie realmes by thy vertue and battaile, and by those feates by which thie Father attamed both his adversaries and thine.[3]

In 1513 or 1514 a translation of the work of Tito Livio was offered by an unnamed writer to King Henry VIII because he had "now of late entered into semblable warr against the Frenchmen." [4] The translator inserted moralizations throughout the course of the narrative, and Kingsford says of these insertions:

> They are the endeavour of an historian to draw instruction from the past for the benefit of the present. Their didactic purpose was not purely moral; there is in them a deliberate design to apply the political lesson of the life of Henry V to the times of Henry VIII.[5]

It is thus evident that the life of Henry V was first written as a mirror of victorious deeds for his son, and that it grew into "the first English life of King Henry the Fifth" in order that it might serve as a mirror to Henry VIII in a "semblable warr." Holinshed and Stow both consulted Tito Livio, Kingsford says, and Halle did not.[6] But the theme of all the chroniclers was the same, for Halle took as the title for the section of his chronicle dealing with this hero-king "The victorious actes of kyng Henry the V." The play upon which Shakespeare drew for a selection of incidents had likewise the title of *The Famous Victories of Henry V*.[7] It was predetermined that in writing about Henry V Shakespeare should write about war and victory in war, as

[2] C. L. Kingsford, *The First English Life of King Henry the Fifth* (Oxford, 1911), pp. xiv-xv, and xlvi.

[3] *Ibid.*, 7. The quotation is from the 1513 English translation.

[4] *Ibid.*, 190.

[5] *Ibid.*, xiii.

[6] *Ibid.*, xlvi.

[7] See *ibid.*, pp. xlvii-lvi for a discussion of the relation of the first *Life* to this play and to Shakespeare's *Henry V*. The most complete study is B. M. Ward's "*The Famous Victories of Henry V:* Its Place in Elizabethan Dramatic Literature," *Review of English Studies*, IV (1928), 270-94.

it had been that in writing about Henry IV he should write about rebellion. In the midst of his wooing of the Princess Katherine of France, Henry V, indeed, explains his stern visage by the fact that his father "was thinking of civil wars when he got me." [8]

The Elizabethan period was, by and large, a time of peace, for there were no wars with foreign invaders fought on English soil; yet the English fought in Scotland and in Ireland, in France on behalf of Henry IV, and in the Netherlands on behalf of the Lowlanders against Spain. Elizabeth had an army as well as a navy ready to meet invasion at the time of the Armada, and she continued to be troubled by fears of an invasion long afterward, especially during 1598, when Henry IV of France was making peace with Spain in spite of English protests, and in 1599, when Camden says an army was called up, ostensibly at least to meet a Spanish threat.[9] Professor Dietz estimates that Elizabeth, up to 1588, spent for military purposes £1,517,351, and from that time on very much more. Between 1585 and 1596 she spent in aiding the Netherlands £1,186,119, and Henry IV of France was in her debt £445,125 when she tried to effect a settlement with him.[10] If we consider the value of money at that time and the comparatively small population, we realize that such expenditures for war, added to the constant raising of forces to fight on land and on sea, must have kept war to the forefront of English interests throughout the reign, as indeed it did. The useful bibliography of English and continental books on military matters by Captain Cockle gives ample proof that England was not only reading but quarreling about the theories and the arts of war.[11]

When Shakespeare wrote *Henry V,* then, does not concern us if we regard it as simply a political play about war, war viewed from the Elizabethan point of view. But from Simpson [12] onward there has

[8] *Henry V,* V, ii, 238-39.

[9] Camden, *Historie of the . . . Princesse Elizabeth,* Bk. IV, 142-43. Camden implies that the rumors concerning the Earl of Essex constituted the real reason.

[10] F. C. Dietz, *English Public Finance, 1558-1641* (New York and London, 1932, for the American Historical Association), 59, 455, 459.

[11] M. J. D. Cockle, *A Bibliography of English Military Books up to 1642 and of Contemporary Foreign Works* (London, 1900).

[12] Richard Simpson, "The Political Use of the Stage in Shakespeare's Time" and "The Politics of Shakespeare's Historical Plays," *The New Shakespeare Society's Transactions* (1874), 416-419; see E. M. Albright, "The Folio Version of *Henry V* in Relation to Shakespeare's Times," *PMLA,* XLIII (1928), 722-56.

been a tendency to associate the play with Essex. The facts are these. The first quarto, a "bad" quarto, was published in 1600. Meres failed to mention *Henry V* in his *Palladis Tamia* in 1598, and he did mention *Henry IV*. The chorus that precedes the fifth act of *Henry V* makes obvious reference to the expected victorious return of Essex from Ireland, where he had gone to quell rebellion in March, 1599, and must have been written after that date and before September of that year, when the harried earl made his very unvictorious appearance in England. But the choruses, certain scenes, and many passages of dialogue did not appear in the quartos, being first printed in the folio of 1623. Chambers thinks that the play, choruses and all, was probably written in 1599, but any conclusions that go beyond these facts must remain tentative.[13] Those who regard Henry V as Essex, however, make two mistakes, it seems to me. In the first place, Shakespeare does not compare Essex to Henry V; what he compares is the greeting which would be given to Essex if he should return from Ireland, "Bringing rebellion broached on his sword," to the greeting which Henry V received from the populace when he returned victorious from France. In the second place, even though Essex were compared to Henry V in the chorus, it would be a mistake to assume that he must therefore be Henry V throughout the play. It is the mistake which critics have made, who, finding Duessa certainly presenting the case of Mary Stuart in the trial scene of Book V of the *Faerie Queene,* try to make Duessa represent Mary Stuart throughout the whole poem. The result is confusion, for that is not the way of the artist who holds his mirror up to nature. Undoubtedly Shakespeare here as elsewhere had specific and contemporary situations in mind, but he does not simply label a contemporary character with an historical name. Even the situations and the roles of Mary and her son James of Scotland were merged in the picture of Arthur in *King John,* by far the most specific of the historical mirrors.

Henry V is apparently based on Holinshed and covers the period from Lent, 1414, to May, 1420. The character and the achievements of the king remain true to tradition, though both persons and times are frequently telescoped. During this period the dauphin of France was first Lewis, then John, then Charles. To Shakespeare he is merely

[13] For a full discussion of these matters see E. K. Chambers, *William Shakespeare,* I, 395.

the dauphin. Henry's war upon France is abridged and compressed. The Battle of Agincourt in 1415 is followed by the peacemaking at Troyes in 1420, only the chorus to Act V bridging the years. This chorus takes the king to London by way of Calais and boldly declares that the play omits "All the occurrences, whatever chanc'd,/Till Harry's back-return again to France." The great battles fought on his return to France in 1417 are, however, omitted, so that we are left to infer that the French made peace because of the victory at Agincourt. The peace parley at Troyes in 1420 is apparently telescoped with the meeting at Meulan in 1419, where Henry fell in love with the Princess Katherine.[14] There is also much in the play that is not in the chronicles, but, as I have said, the general picture remains true to the pattern set by Tito Livio and continued in all the English chronicles. . . .

[14] W. G. Boswell-Stone, *Shakspere's Holinshed* (New York, 1896), pp. 165 *et seq.*

Introduction to *Henry V*

by Geoffrey Bullough

Henry the Fifth was probably first performed between March and September, 1599, while Essex was in Ireland. It was not mentioned by Francis Meres in *Palladis Tamia* (1598). An entry in *S.R.* on 4 August, 1600, describes the play as one of several 'to be staied', i.e. not to be published without permission from the Lord Chamberlain's Company who owned the right text. However, a pirated version (Q1) was printed by Thomas Creede for Thomas Millington and John Busby in 1600. On 14 August in the same year an entry in *S.R.* notes the right of Thomas Pavyer to the copy, but the second Quarto, which Creede printed for Pavyer in 1602, was set up from Q1, as was Q3, published in 1619 by William Jaggard but with 'Printed for T.P. 1608' on the title-page.

F1 is the most reliable of the texts. The relation of Q1 to it has caused controversy. 'If Q1 is read side by side with F1', (wrote Chambers), 'it is impossible to regard it as anything but a continual perversion of the same text.' On the other hand Pollard and Wilson treated Q1 as based on an old play already existent before 1593, when it was partly revised by Shakespeare, 'transcribed in an abridged form for provincial use in 1593, and finally printed partly from this transcript and partly from an actor's report of a performance of the play as further revised by Shakespeare from the original manuscript' (*WSh* 1.393–4). If this were true, Q1 must in part represent a source-play; but although one must admire the ingenuity of Pollard and Wilson's reasoning, their theory does not make clear what parts of Q1 are 'old play'. Since 'the original play . . . is taken to have been itself a revision of *The Famous Victories*' (Chambers), I have thought it best to confine my attention to that play as printed in 1598, while recognizing that the original *Famous Victories* may have been longer than it is now, and that more than one stage of writing may have come between that and our *Henry V*.[1]

Actually there is more connection between *Henry V* and *Famous Victories* than between the latter and *Henry IV*. There are many significant resemblances, and although much of the common material was inevitable in any play founded on the chronicles, there can be little doubt that Shakespeare recalled both the structure of the last half of *Famous Victories* (Sc. ix-xx; *supra* 321ff) and some of its incidents, historical and unhistorical. Both plays omit the Lollard unrest and other domestic events, and both make a great scene of the English claim to France, and discuss whether France or Scotland should be attacked first. Immediately afterwards the French ambassador delivers the 'tennis-balls' challenge, which Henry takes in almost identical words, not suggested by Hall or Holinshed:

FV 846 My lord prince Dolphin is very pleasant with me.
H5 I.2.259. We are glad the Dauphin is so pleasant with us.

Both plays then shift to the common people of London, showing three different types of army-recruit (*FV* Sc.x; *H5* II.1). Both show the parting of husband and wife as comic (*FV* Sc.x; *H5* II.3). Both then show the French court remarking on the reception of the embassage to England (*FV* Sc. xi; *H5* II.4). *Famous Victories* in its present mutilated state omits the Siege of Harfleur but alludes to it in five lines (Sc. xii) in a way which suggests that originally the Siege was shown (cf. *H5* III. 1, 2, 3). In each play fun is derived from the differences between the French and English languages (*FV* in the dicing Scene xiii; *H5* with Katharine learning English in III.4). Inevitably, following the Chronicles, there is much coming and going of heralds, messengers, etc. (*FV* Sc. xii, xiv; *H5* III.6; IV.3, 7). Both plays show the encounter of an unheroic English clown with a French soldier (*FV* Sc. xvii; *H5* IV,4); both present matter connected with looting (*FV* Sc. xix; *H5* III.2, 6); and discussions of how to live when dis-

[1] Cf. E. A. Morgan's suggestion that *FV* and the Shakespeare trilogy were based on an earlier play now lost (*Some Problems of Shakespeare's Henry IV*, 1924).

banded (*FV ibid.; H5* V.1). Both plays move from Agincourt to the Treaty of Troyes, omitting the second invasion of France. Each has a royal wooing scene in which the King shows blunt joviality (*FV* xviii; *H5* V.2). The conduct of the peace negotiations is similar in both plays (*FV* Sc. xviii, xx; *H5* V.2).

Some of these parallels are not close or sustained; some were to be expected in any Elizabethan treatment of the theme. Nevertheless it can hardly be doubted that in writing *Henry V* Shakespeare was affected both positively (to accept) and negatively (to reject and replace) material found in the original of *Famous Victories*. But he transmuted almost everything that he touched, and although his Henry V retains some of the bluff, blunt masculinity of the earlier drama, he gives him a high seriousness, a religious sense of responsibility, entirely lacking there, and also infuses the major scenes with a heroic quality unequalled even in his own earlier Histories.

The reign of Henry V had long been regarded as one mainly of 'Victorious Acts' (so Hall headed his chapter), as the king sought peace through war and 'rest with victorie . . . by [his] vertue and battaile' (Titus Livius). The sixteenth century regarded his French claims as just, and his actions as altogether admirable both before and during his invasion. He behaved always in the best chivalric tradition, and his youthful escapades seemed all the more endearing when he became, as Holinshed declared, 'a majestie . . . that both lived and died a paterne in princehood, a lode-starre in honour, and mirrour of magnificence'.

All tended therefore to encourage Shakespeare to develop in this play the nobler aspects of his Faulconbridge in *King John* so as to present the hero-king in action as the climax of his dramatic sequence on kingship. But *Henry V* goes further than it need in the direction of epic-drama. Indeed Shakespeare seems to have felt that his theatrical technique was inadequate to his subject. Not that his material itself was too episodic for drama. By compressing the reign into what is virtually one campaign (as did *Famous Victories*) and closely following Agincourt with the successful peace negotiations of five years afterwards, he made his play less fragmentary than *King John* or *Henry VI*. But he obviously believed that the subject deserved epic rather than dramatic treatment. No doubt his reading of the Chronicles and the traditional fame of the monarch who had conquered most of

France gave him this idea. But it is likely that his fancy gained support from Samuel Daniel, whose *Civile Wars* he had already used to good effect for *Richard II* and for Hal's youth in *Henry IV*. Daniel himself could not tell of Henry V's victories, since he was limited to relating (as he states)

> 'in lamentable verse
> Nothing but bloudshed, treasons, sin and shame'

He could include from this glorious reign only the wretched conspiracy of Richard Earl of Cambridge, and that he treated summarily with incredible feebleness. But recognizing the poetic possibilities of the period Daniel began his Fourth Book [Text V] by raising the King's ghost to lament the lack of an English epic on himself and other English warriors of his age:

> O what eternall matter here is found!
> Whence new immortal *Iliads* might proceed (6)

(cries the ghost, and)

> O that our times had had some sacred wight
> Whose wordes as happie as our swordes had bin
> To have prepar'd for us *Tropheis* aright
> Of undecaying frames t'have rested in. (8)

He hopes that Queen Elizabeth will order her poets ('bright ornaments to us denide') to 'get our ruyn'd deedes re-edifide' in an immortal poem.

Daniel's own panegyric of Henry V follows the portrait in Hall and Holinshed, describes him as 'Mirror of vertue, miracle of worth', and insists on his powers of leadership and discipline (17, 18), his bringing 'distracted discontent' into a unity of warlike action. Only the treacherous attempt of the Earl of Cambridge marred the domestic peace of a reign marked by justice and order. Daniel was not at his best in this part of his poem, but his remarks not only show that Henry V was regarded as a good ruler at home as well as a conqueror abroad but also reflect an unusual awareness of England's shortcomings in heroic poetry—a lack which neither Daniel nor Drayton—with his Agincourt poem—was able to repair.

Writing a few years after Daniel Shakespeare was also conscious of the need for 'a Muse of fire, that would ascend/The brightest heaven of invention'. Since the form imposed upon him was drama he yearned for a theatre with

> A kingdom for a stage, princes to act
> And monarchs to behold the swelling scene.

As it was he must do his best with the Globe or Curtain stage, and the ability of the audience to 'Piece out our imperfections with your thoughts'. Whereas Ben Jonson in the Prologue to *Every Man in His Humour* complained of the sprawling manner of romantic plays and histories, Shakespeare regretted that his play and stage could not include enough, with its 'Turning the accomplishment of many years/ Into an hour-glass'. Accordingly he inserted a Chorus before each Act and added an Epilogue, using them to arouse a sublime feeling of patriotic exaltation and urgency in the audience, to apologize for the stage's shortcomings and at the same time to remedy them by linking the episodes (adding also descriptions of places and incidents not to be represented), to excite suspense about future events, and generally to dignify and elevate the action with heroic glamour.[1] In short, Shakespeare was making an experiment in epic-drama in which, while recognizing the limitations of the theatre, he overcame them by employing a compère to supply epic spaciousness, detachment and sublimity. It rose indeed nearer to epic-tone than anything Daniel or Drayton ever wrote.

Shakespeare's main historical source was Holinshed, who followed Hall closely, compressing his account but supplementing his predecessor with material drawn from elsewhere. Where 'the significant words and phrases are in both' (Walter),[2] as in I.2.75–81, the source is probably Holinshed's shortened version; otherwise one might expect to find occasional departures from his details. Sometimes the play agrees with Holinshed in including matter not in Hall. Thus Hall does not say that the countermining of the French at Harfleur 'somewhat disappointed the Englishmen' (cf. III.2.58–65), nor does Hall mention the wish (ascribed by Shakespeare to Westmoreland in IV.3.16–18) that they had ten thousand more men (cf. *inf.* p. 394); he omits the Constable's taking a banner from a trumpet and fasten-

[1] Cf. J. Munro, Introduction to *H5, The London Shakespeare,* 1958, IV.1018.
[2] *New Arden,* ed. J. H. Walter, 1954.

ing it on his spear (IV.2.61–2), and the King's threat to the French cavalry (IV.7.54–64).

Nevertheless there are clear signs that the dramatist used Hall as well as Holinshed and that he may have had them both open by his side as he wrote some parts of his play. Thus he follows Hall in placing the tennis-balls incident (I.2) after, not before, the proroguing of Parliament, thereby making Henry's determination to invade France depend not on pique but on the Archbishop's reasoned statement of his claims. In writing of a 'tun' of 'tennis balls' he follows Hall, or *Famous Victories* (which used Hall); the phrase 'meeter for your spirit', however, (254) probably comes from Holinshed's phrase 'more meet'; the reference by Henry to his 'wilder days' (267) probably returns to Hall. The allusion to 'gunstones' (282) appears in neither Hall nor Holinshed, but may be a reminiscence of Caxton's version of the Brut Chronicle (1482) where Henry 'lete make tenys balles for the dolphyn in al the hast that they myght be made, and they were harde and grete gunne-stones for the Dolphyn to playe with-alle'.

A few other illustrations may be desirable. An allusion to Hall's description of Henry IV's reign as an 'unquiet time' appears at the beginning of the play (I.1.4). In I.2, although Canterbury's historical detail closely follows Holinshed, the debate owes something to Hall. For instance, in I.2.100–24, the Archbishop's references to Edward III and the Black Prince and the exhortations of Ely and Exeter to 'awake remembrance of these valiant dead' expand Hall's 'diminishe not youre title, which youre noble progenitors so highly have estemed' (not found in Holinshed). From Hall comes Canterbury's assertion that 'they of the marches' will be adequate to defend the north against the Scots (140–3); in *Famous Victories* (773) the Archbishop advises Henry to attack Scotland before France. Exeter's warning about the bereavements of war (II.4.105–9) may also derive from Hall (*inf.* 401n.). Hall made the French leaders discuss English habits of eating and drinking (*sup.* 332). Shakespeare may have recalled this at III.5.18–19 and 7.153–9, though both *Famous Victories* (1135) and *Henry VI Part 1* (I.2.7–12), had used the passage. Henry's reference to the man who sold the lion's skin before killing it (IV.3.90–4) was probably suggested by Hall's reference to the 'phantasticall braggynge' of the French. Minor hints also came from Fabyan and Stow. The discussion about Scotland in I.2 may owe a little to a passage in Hardyng's *Chronicle* where the poet, who served at the Courts of Henry VI and Edward IV is urging the latter to bring back his defeated predecessor from Scotland, by invading and conquering that country, to which he has a rightful claim:

> Considre also, moste earthly soveraigne Lorde
> Of French not Scottes ye get never to your paie
> Any treaty of trewce, or good concorde
> But if it bee under your banner aye
> Whiche maie never bee—by reason any waie
> But if your realme stande well in unitee
> Conserved well, in peace and equitee.
>
> Your Marches kept, and also your sea full clere
> To Fraunce or Spaine, ye maie ride for your right
> To Portyngale and Scotland with your banner
> Whils your rereward in England standeth wight
> Under your banner, your enemies will you hight
> A better treaty, within a litle date
> Then in four yere, to your ambassate. (1543 edn. f.231v)

Of the fifteenth-century sources for the life of Henry V, most of them unpublished in the sixteenth century, Shakespeare may have known none directly; but interesting parallels have been drawn, especially by J. D. Wilson. Fluellen's statement that the 'pax' stolen by Bardolph was 'of little price' (III.6.46) resembles that by the chaplain in Henry's army who wrote in his *Gesta Henrici Quinti* (soon after Agincourt) of a soldier who 'had stolen a pyx of gilded copper, perhaps he thought it was gold'. Similarly Gower's 'The enemy is loud' (IV.1.76) on the night before Agincourt is anticipated by the chaplain who writes 'we heard the enemy shouting'; this is in Caxton and implied by Hall and Holinshed. The *Gesta* gives the total of the English army as 'not more than 6,000' (cf. IV.3.76, 'five thousand men'), whereas Holinshed gives 15,000.

In the *Vita et Gesta Henrici Quinti* once ascribed to Thomas of Elmham, Scrope's treason is ascribed to 'diabolical suggestion' (cf. II.2.111–2)—but is this unusual? The same work declares that Henry kissed Princess Katharine at their meeting at Melun (cf. V.2.258–86); but a kiss would be the natural climax of the wooing-scene. More striking is the pseudo-Elmham's account of Henry's change of heart as caused by grief and repentance after his father's death, when 'he is converted by a happy miracle'. This agrees with Canterbury's wonder in I.1.24–37 at the suddenness of the Prince's transformation. Shakespeare had already shown the Prince as needing little alteration to become the ideal king. For dramatic effect at the start of his new play he probably based Canterbury's description on Holinshed's assertion that Henry 'determined to put on him the shape of a new man' (*supra* 280 taken from Hall, *supra* 286). Compare Fabyan's account:

> 'This man before the death of his father, applyed him unto all vyce and insolency, and drewe unto him all riottours and wildly disposed persons. But after he was admitted to the rule of the lande, anon and sodainely he became a newe man, and turned all that rage and wildenesse into sobernesse and wise sadnesse, and the vice into constant vertue. And for he would continewe that vertue, and not to be reduced ther unto by the familiaritie of his old nise company, he therfore after rewardes to them geven, charged them upon paine of their lives, that none of them were so hardy as to come within x. mile of suche place as he were lodged in, after a day by him assigned.' (*Chronicle,* 1559, p. 389)

In the additions to his *Chronicles* made in the *Annales* (1592), Stow made Henry confess himself to 'a certaine monke of holie conversation'. Clearly the tradition was, as Hardyng put it, that

> The houre he was crowned and anoynt
> He chaunged was, of al his olde condicion . . .
> A newe man made, by al good regimence.

The *Vita Henrici Quinti* by 'Titus Livius', in the English version augmented by its translator (1513), reveals certain parallels, such as the Frenchmen's boasts about their horses and armour (cf. III.7), and the King's habit of inspecting his army. Holinshed alludes to this characteristic of Henry V, though less vividly. Maybe Shakespeare took the hint from him, and developed it from a classical parallel in Tacitus, as we shall see.[1] The description of the King's arrival in Dover (Act V, Chorus 9–20) has something in common with a passage in the Latin *Life,* but the resemblance seems generic rather than specific.

[1] In *The True Tragedie of Richard III* (1594) before the Battle of Bosworth Oxford reproves Richmond for 'these night walkes and scouting abroad in the evenings so disguised'. But Richmond's purpose was different (cf. III, 336-7).

Shakespeare was probably drawing on Stow (who owned a copy of the work) to supplement Hall and Holinshed.

Shakespeare picks his way through Holinshed's numerous detail, limiting himself mainly to the French business, omitting most happenings in England and ignoring the conflict with the Lollards and the execution of Sir John Oldcastle. He divides his material so as to suggest a climax at the end of each act. Thus Act I extends from the statement of the King's claim to the French throne to his resolution to invade France; Act II extends from the Cambridge conspiracy to the French realization that Henry has arrived to avenge their insults; Act III traces events from the landing and investment of Harfleur to the eve before Agincourt; Act IV includes the battle and victory; Act V treats of the peace conference at Troyes, the King's wooing of Princess Katharine, and the preparation for the union of the two crowns. So the whole drama is organized round the heroic strife between England and France, and after the triumph at Agincourt the historical events of 1416–19 are omitted or telescoped in order to hasten the acceptance of the King's claim and his marriage.

As in *Henry IV* two strands, political and social, are interwoven so as to make England as well as its epic representative the subject of his play. We see Henry V as the ideal man of action, reasonable, just, touched with some of his old impetuosity, but now entirely devoted to the service of his country, and aware of his grave responsibilities. But he is not a king *in vacuo;* he is King of Britain, surrounded by men of all types and classes, churchmen, nobles, an army of common folk, soldiers willing and unwilling, good and bad, grave and gay, Welshmen, Irishmen and Scots, who participate variously in his war; and he has his enemies at home as well as in France. To present this varied picture of a dutiful monarch and a people on the march the dramatist draws not only from Holinshed and other chroniclers but also from the latter part of *Famous Victories*.

PART TWO

Interpretations

Henry V

by Charles Williams

With *Henry V,* therefore, Shakespeare reached the climax of exterior life; it is at once a conclusion and a beginning. It is not primarily a patriotic play, for the First Chorus knows nothing of patriotism nor of England, but only of *a Muse of fire which would ascend the brightest heaven of invention* by discovering a challenge between mighty monarchies. Patriotism certainly keeps breaking in, but rather like the army itself: the mass behind Henry is dramatically an English mass, and as the play proceeds he becomes more and more an English king. So much must be allowed to the patriots; it is, however, for them to allow that he becomes something else and more as well, and it is in that something more that his peculiar strength lies.

Before defining that, however, and his own words define it, it may be well to remark a few of the differences between *Henry V* and its precedent *Henry IV*. The newer manner of the blank verse itself is accentuated; it gains in speed. Less even than in *Henry IV* are there any involutions or adornments; its movements, like the action of the persons, admit of no delay. It has lost superfluity, though it has not yet gained analysis. No word blurs, but each word does not yet illuminate, as each was to illuminate in that later play of action and vision, *Antony and Cleopatra*. Here it is equivalent to the King's desire and the King's deed, and equals the one with the other. But there is, at first, no variation between the King and other characters, as there is variation between the Prince and Hotspur and Falstaff in *Henry IV:* what the King is, he is, and the others are apart from him. In

"Henry V," by Charles Williams. From Shakespeare Criticism 1919-1935, *ed. by Anne Ridler (London: Oxford University Press, 1936).*

fact, the next differences between the two plays are (i) the omission of Hotspur, and (ii) the omission of Falstaff. It will be said that Hotspur is dead before *Henry IV* ends and Falstaff dies soon after *Henry V* begins. But whatever historical necessity or moral convenience compelled those two deaths, the result is to leave the stage free not only for King Henry himself, but for something else—for the development of the idea of honour. In *Henry IV* honour had been peculiarly the property of Hotspur, and it had seemed like being his property in a narrower sense. He had regarded it almost as if it were something he owned as he owned his armour, something that he could capture and possess.

> By heaven methinks it were an easy leap
> To pluck bright honour from the pale-fac'd moon,
> Or dive into the bottom of the deep,
> Where fathom-line could never touch the ground,
> And pluck up drowned honour by the locks;
> So he that doth redeem her thence might wear
> Without corrival all her dignities:

Against this splendid and egotistical figure is the figure of Falstaff. Up to the last act of *2 Henry IV* the distinction of Falstaff had been that, though he may want a lot for his comfort, he does not need it for his complacency. Hotspur, without a sense of his own honour, feels himself deficient; it is why he rebels. Falstaff, without the same sense, feels himself free; it is why he runs away or fights as circumstances and his own common sense dictate. Henry V might have been made like either of them; in fact, he was made like neither. Neither Hotspur nor Falstaff could suit the Muse of fire or the brightest heaven. Honour must for Henry in his own play be something consonant with that brightness, and that invention discovered a phrase which made honour more than reputation—whether for possession or repudiation.

> And those that leave their valiant bones in France,
> Dying like men, though buried in your dunghills,
> They shall be fam'd; for there the sun shall greet them,
> And draw their honours reeking up to heaven,
> Leaving their earthly parts to choke your clime.

Their bodies are dead; their honours live, but not as fame upon earth. The heaven of invention is to suggest this other heaven; the honour of poetry is to show the honour of the spirit in challenge. It is a little reminiscent of *Lycidas;* where also Fame is transmuted into something pleasing to 'all-judging Jove.' The honours which so live are the spirits and souls of the righteous—anyhow, of the righteous at Agincourt. It is to Henry that the identification is given; it is for him that honour is now a name for man's immortal part. If that venture of war which is the result of the challenge between two great worldly powers, two mighty monarchies, is defeated, this end at least is left to those who carry themselves well in that venture.

As far as the war itself is concerned, the play did not attempt any illusion. It put war 'in the round.' The causes of it are there; dynastic claims are the equivalent of the modern prestige of governments. The force of the verse carries the sincerity of the intention, and the tennis-balls are part of the cause of the war; that is, the other monarchy is also involved. Any insincerity is part of the way of things, but insufficient to cloud the glory of the change. In this sense Shakespeare threw over the diplomatic advice of the King in *Henry IV* as well as the martial egotism of Hotspur.

Besides the causes of war there is, in the first Harfleur scene, what a soldier-poet called 'Joy of Battle'; so, with a horrid faithfulness, in the second Harfleur scene, is the usual result of Joy of Battle. So, finally, in the field before Agincourt, is a kind of summing-up. War is not so very much more dangerous than peace; one is almost as likely to be killed one way as the other. 'Every soldier's duty is the King's, but every subject's soul is his own', which if he keep clean, it does not very much matter whether he lives or dies. Death is not all that important—to Henry (who in the play was going to fight), to the lords, to the army, and, as a consequence, to the citizens of Harfleur. The Duke of Burgundy's oration in the last Act describes all the general advantages of peace, but it does not do more. Peace, as a general thing, is preferable to war, but life is pretty dangerous any way—pretty bloody, in every sense of the word—and a healthy male adult should be prepared for death at any moment. So what does it matter? It is not the modern view, but we are not Elizabethans, and our police are efficient.

Honour then—the capacity to challenge the world and to endure the result of challenge—is the state to be coveted.

> But if it be a sin to covet honour,
> I am the most offending soul alive.

Those lines come from the most famous of Henry's speeches. But there is another and much shorter and less famous speech which throws a stronger light on Henry. There had been a minor crisis—the conspiracy in the Second Act—before the great crisis of Agincourt. But as no one has the least interest in the Lord Scroop of Masham, and as no one can feel the King himself has had time to love him behind the scenes either in *Henry IV* or *Henry V*, the conspiracy fails to excite. We are left to listen to the King being merely vocal. When, however, the central crisis approached, Shakespeare had another way of being equivalent to it. This comes in the English camp by night before the battle, very soon after the greatest thing in the play, the sublime Fourth Chorus. In that Chorus a change had been presented as coming over the whole war. The venture had gone wrong, the challenge delivered to the world of the French had been accepted and that French world had trapped the English army and was on the point of destroying it. At the point of that pause the Fourth Chorus delivers its speech, describing the night, the gloom, and the danger. But its speech, if the words are literally followed, has two futures. The first is Agincourt; the second is the tragedies. There is not only a change in *Henry V;* there is a still darker change away from *Henry V*. The Muse of fire has been ascending her heaven—that is the poetry's own description of what it has been trying to do. But now it directly suggests that it is doing something quite different.

> Now entertain conjecture of a time
> When creeping murmur and the poring dark
> Fills the wide vessel of the universe.

The word 'universe' means, certainly, earth and heaven in that darkness before the battle. But there seems no reason why it should not also mean 'universe' in the accepted sense, the whole world and the whole heaven, including the brightest heaven of poetry with which we began. It is all this which is beginning to be filled with creeping murmur and the poring dark. Poetry and (so to speak) life are being occupied by this universal noise and night. It is not yet so fixed; it is but a guess and a wonder. 'Now entertain conjecture—' It is the prelude to all the plays that were to come.

From poetry thus conceiving of its own probable business, both locally at Agincourt and universally, and its future, two other enlargements follow. One concerns the English army; the other, the King.

The *Muse of Fire* is compelled to behold the army as 'so many horrid ghosts', and the description of the soldiers is that of men who are in the state she has described. It is an army but it is also humanity. To 'sit patiently and inly ruminate the morning's danger' is a situation familiar enough to us in peace as to them in war, if 'danger' also may be given a wider meaning than that of battle. Illness, unemployment, loneliness, these are the things that make sacrifices of 'the poor condemned English', that make them 'pining and pale'. It is among such a host of spectral images of mankind that the King moves, and the Chorus imagines him as their contrast and support: 'the royal captain of this ruined band'. It remains true, however, that the Chorus has to do this without having had, up to that point, much support from the play itself. Henry has been cheerful and efficient and warlike and friendly, but he has not suggested to us his capacity for being an almost supernatural 'little touch of Harry in the night'. The wider and the darker the night, the more that gleam shines. But why?

The cause follows. When the King appears he is speaking, more or less lightly, of the advantages which evil chances bring with them. It is not a particularly original remark, not a moment of 'great insight', and we need not perhaps suppose it is meant to be solemn or serious. It is in the next speech that the sudden difference between Henry and all the rest appears.

> 'Tis good for men to love their present pains
> Upon example; so the spirit is eas'd:
> And when the mind is quicken'd, out of doubt,
> The organs, though defunct and dead before,
> Break up their drowsy grave, and newly move
> With casted slough and fresh legerity.

This is the centre of Henry's capacity. He 'loves' his present pains, and his spirit is therefore eased. He has rather more than accepted darkness, danger, defeat, and death, and loves them. It is this which gives him a new quickening of the mind, new motions of the organs; it destroys sloth and the drowsy grave of usual life. It is this love and the resulting legerity of spirit which enable him to be what the Chorus describe, and what the rest of the Act accentuates.

> Upon his royal face there is no note
> How dread an army hath enrounded him;

how can there be when he loves being enrounded?

> But freshly looks and overbears attaint
> With cheerful semblance and sweet majesty.

It is precisely a description of what he has done within himself. Therefore every wretch 'plucks comfort from his looks', receiving the 'largess universal' from his liberal eye—from the eased spirit, the quickened mind, the moving organs, which are the effect of his love for present pains.

Perhaps this also was something of the explanation of the dead Falstaff; perhaps Henry was more like his old acquaintance than he altogether knew. Only the word 'love' can hardly be used of Falstaff in any sense; it was by no accident or haste that Shakespeare could not show him in more 'love' than the odd possibility of lechery excites. He enjoyed his dilemmas in the sense that he enjoyed being equal to them, but Henry enjoys them because he is careless of them.

There is a distinction, and it lies in the fact that the King's spirit is 'honour' whereas Falstaff's is the rejection of 'honour'. It also lies in the fact that Falstaff does die when he cannot conquer 'the King's unkindness'. If ever Falstaff's spirit was drawn reeking up to heaven, he would only enter it on his own terms, but Henry will enter it on Heaven's terms. It is Falstaff's greatness that we are delighted to feel heaven give way to him; Henry's that we are eased by his giving way to heaven. But the artistic difference is that there is no more to be done in the method of Falstaff—he is complete and final. He can be continually varied and repeated, but he cannot be developed. Henry is complete, but not final. For he, in whose honour there is no self-contradiction, could love his pains simply because there was nothing else to do except run away, and that the same honour forbade. The genius of Shakespeare proceeded, however, immediately to imagine an honour in which self-contradiction did passionately exist; it emerged as Brutus, and was set in front of a power which was more 'monstrous' than that of the French army; he called that monstrosity Caesar, and made another play out of those other conditions, in which the crisis is a more deeply interior thing, and the heaven of honour begins itself to be at odds.

Henry then has made of his crisis an exaltation of his experience; he has become gay. This gaiety—a 'modest' gaiety, to take another adjective from the Chorus—lasts all through the Act. It lightens and saves the speech on ceremony; more especially, it illuminates the speech to Westmoreland. In view of the King's capacity the stress there may well be on the adjective rather than the substantive: 'We few, we *happy* few'. His rejection of all those who have no stomach for the fight, his offer of crowns for convoy, is part of the same delight: so far as possible he will have no one there who does not love to be there. He makes jokes at the expense of the old men's 'tall stories' of the battle, and at the French demand for ransom. We are clean away from the solemn hero-king, and therefore much more aware of the Harry of the Chorus, and of the thing he is—the 'touch of Harry in the night'. The very last line of that scene—'how thou pleasest, God, dispose the day'—is not a prayer of resignation but a cry of complete carelessness. What does it matter what *happens?*

It is a legerity of spirit, the last legerity before the tragedies. Hamlet was to have a touch of it, but there is little else, in the greater figures, until, as from beyond a much greater distance, it is renewed by a phrase Kent uses of the Fool in *Lear*. Who, says a Gentleman on the moor, is with the King?

> None but the Fool, who labours to outjest
> His heart-struck injuries.

Henry's injuries are not heart-struck; he is no tragic figure. But he deserves more greatly than has perhaps always been allowed. The Muse, *entertaining conjecture* of a new and dreadful world, conjectured also a touch in the night, the thawing of fear, a royal captain of a ruined band, and conjectured the nature of the power of love and consequent lightness that thrills through the already poring dusk.

Henry V

by E. M. W. Tillyard

I have conjectured that Hall's chronicle caught Shakespeare's youthful imagination and impelled him to dramatize the whole stretch of English history from the prosperity of Edward III, through the disasters that succeeded, to the establishment of civil peace under the Tudors. In all the History Plays so far written (*King John* excepted, which is outside the sequence) he had fulfilled his obligation. But in the last three plays he had quite exceeded it by giving, concurrently with the strict historical theme, his epic picture of medieval and of contemporary England. But this excess could not cancel the residue of his obligation. He had created his picture of the great traditional villain king; he had still to create his picture of the great hero king. Richard III had figured in *2* and *3 Henry VI* and had declared his character. But that was not enough. Hall, by incorporating More's life of Richard III, dwells on that king with a special emphasis. Shakespeare fulfils his obligation to Hall by giving Richard a play to himself, in which his monstrosity is done full justice to. Hall, following the tradition established by Polydore Vergil, makes Henry V the second exceptional figure in his chronicle: the copy-book paragon of kingly virtue, to balance Richard the monstrous pattern of concentrated vice. If Shakespeare was to carry his work through he was obliged to treat Henry like Richard: to allow him a play to himself. There was a personal reason why Shakespeare should not acquiesce in the precedent of Hall: he had finished the theme of England or Respublica and was almost forced to allow a concrete hero to dominate his next History Play.

But Shakespeare also had his duty to the expectations of an Elizabethan audience. Having achieved popularity in showing Henry's youthful dissipation he could not, without scandal, refuse to show Henry in his traditional part of perfect king. And this traditional part contained factors not found in Hall: namely his sudden miraculous conversion when he came to the throne and his pre-eminence among English kings as the bluff hearty man and the good mixer. The legend of his conversion was powerful and of long standing. It began with the chronicler Walsingham, who said that Henry on coming to the throne was turned suddenly into another man, and persisted in the *Famous Victories of Henry V,* where only a miracle can account for the abrupt transition from waster to serious monarch. The tradition of good mixer finds typical expression in the king's dealing with Simon Eyre in Dekker's *Shoemaker's Holiday*.

Here then were two obligations; and they were both impossible of worthy fulfilment. In creating his epic of England Shakespeare had set himself an exacting standard. His political hero, to be worthy of the standard just set, must be the symbol of some great political principle. And there was no principle he could symbolise. The pre-eminently successful political hero in great literature is Aeneas; and it was Virgil's powerful and steady belief in the missionary and civilising destiny of Rome that animated him. England had not yet reached the stage of Virgil's Rome. She had preserved herself, had achieved union, had "rested true" to herself, but she did not yet stand consciously for any wide political idea. The Tudors were successful by personal astuteness rather than by exemplifying any principle. They were not for export, not oecumenical, thus Henry V, who could at best stand for Elizabethan political principle, could only fail when great weight was put on him. In other words Shakespeare for his hero was obliged ultimately to choose *homo* not *rex*. It is interesting that Milton did precisely the same when he rejected his political hero Arthur for his universal hero Adam. A further difficulty was that the sophisticated, eminently courtly, and not at all exclusively English character whom Shakespeare had created in Prince Hal had no connection at all with the inhuman copybook hero of Polydore Vergil.

To fulfil the second obligation in a manner worthy of the plays he had just written was also impossible. The whole point of the Prince's character was that his conversion was not sudden, that he had been preparing with much deliberation for the coming burden. And as for being the hearty man and the good mixer, the Prince may indeed have charmed his audience by the mere fact of his presence at Eastcheap; but his fundamental detachment and persistent irony are quite at odds with the popular conception of a simple forthright energetic man, transparent in character and separated from simple humble souls only by the accident of his exalted position. It would have been too risky to allow him to remain the ironist after he had come to the throne.

Shakespeare came to terms with this hopeless situation by jettisoning the character he had created and substituting one which, though lacking all consistency, satisfied the requirements both of the chroniclers and of popular tradition. No wonder if the play constructed round him shows a great falling off in quality.

Not that Shakespeare jettisoned his old creation without a struggle. He would hardly have begun his play with

> O for a Muse of fire, that would ascend
> The brightest heaven of invention,

if he had felt quite hopeless of his genius soaring into the empyrean, and thus achieving a miraculous solution of the seemingly impossible. And in the first scene where Henry appears (I. 2) and once or twice later Shakespeare does try to invest his hero with a glamour that shall by its sheer blinding power make us insensible to any inconsistencies. The prelates and nobles who incite Henry to great deeds in France speak splendidly:

> Gracious lord,
> Stand for your own; unwind your bloody flag;
> Look back into your mighty ancestors:
> Go, my dread lord, to your great-grandsire's tomb,
> From whom you claim; invoke his warlike spirit
> And your great-uncle's, Edward the Black Prince,
> Who on the French ground play'd a tragedy,
> Making defeat on the full power of France,
> Whiles his most mighty father on a hill
> Stood smiling to behold his lion's whelp
> Forage in blood of French nobility.

Ely reinforces these words of Canterbury with

> Awake remembrance of these valiant dead
> And with your puissant arm renew their feats.
> You are their heir, you sit upon their throne;
> The blood and courage that renowned them
> Runs in your veins; and my thrice-puissant liege
> Is in the very May-morn of his youth,
> Ripe for exploits and mighty enterprises.

These lines not only dazzle us with their brilliance but they place Henry in the grand context of English history and make us forget the subtle personal touches of his previous character. And they do even more. They refer back to a specific passage in *Henry IV,* the reference to May suggesting the description of Henry and his companions before Shrewsbury,

> As full of spirit as the month of May.

It looks as if Shakespeare was trying desperately, by creating casual links between Prince Hal and Henry V, to mask their fundamental discrepancy. Anyhow we cannot but be appeased for the moment; and when Exeter continues with

> Your brother kings and monarchs of the earth
> Do all expect that you should rouse yourself,
> As did the former lions of your blood,

we are still more appeased, for Exeter here takes up Henry's promise, made at the end of the last play, that he will accept his due place among the other monarchs in the ocean of royalty, that his vanity will no longer beat idly on the rocks but that

> Now doth it turn and ebb back to the sea,
> Where it shall mingle with the state of floods
> And flow henceforth in formal majesty.

Further questionings about Henry's character are held off by Exeter's noble commonplace on the order of government being like music:

> While that the armed hand doth fight abroad,
> The advised head defends itself at home;
> For government, though high and low and lower,

> Put into parts doth keep in one consent,
> Congreeing in a full and natural close,
> Like music—

and by Canterbury's splendid comparison of the state to the beehive. But the truth cannot be withheld for ever and out it comes in Henry's speech to the French ambassador about the tennis balls: a speech whose heavy irony and orotundity compare poorly with the Prince's light ironies and truly Olympian grandeur in *Henry IV*. It is not the same man speaking. Later efforts to inflate Henry to greatness are no more successful. His reproof of the traitor, Lord Scroop, at Southampton, is wonderful poetry, possibly the finest thing in the play; yet it is queerly ineffective in its context. The Henry we knew was an unerring judge of human nature and never gave himself away. When he says of Scroop

> Thou that didst bear the key of all my counsels,
> That knew'st the very bottom of my soul,
> That almost mightst have coin'd me into gold,

he speaks gloriously, he may charm us for the moment, but he ultimately bewilders us. He is utterly inconsistent with his old self and with any of the pieces of self that make up his patchwork character in the present play. Nor can one plead that his words are a sententious passage spoken out of character: they are too emotional. One is tempted to suppose (as nowhere else in all Shakespeare's History Plays) that the poet, defeated in the real business of his drama, is drawing on personal experience and filling up the gap with an account of how someone at some time let him, Shakespeare, down. Once again, Shakespeare tried to save his play in the scenes before Agincourt. Of Henry's conversation with Bates and Williams, Johnson wrote that "the whole argument is well followed, and properly concluded." This is a just comment, but the conversation does not get beyond the sober and the rational. It has the chill of Brutus's speech over Caesar's body rather than the warmth of the prose of the previous plays. Henry's following soliloquy "Upon the king!" is splendid poetry and yet somehow extrinsic to the play, a piece of detached eloquence on a subject on which Shakespeare had long meditated with interest and fervour.

Finally, there is a curious reference back to *Henry IV* near the end of the play, as if even then, when the game was lost, Shakespeare was still hankering after continuity with his late masterpiece. It is where Henry, courting Katharine, mentions his skill in vaulting onto his horse fully armed.

> If I could win a lady at leap-frog, or by vaulting into my saddle with my armour on my back, under correction of bragging be it spoken, I should quickly leap into a wife.

Here is a clear reminiscence of the gay description in *1 Henry IV* . . . of Prince Hal mounting his horse. But how alien the two passages are: the earlier a brilliant piece of Renaissance painting; the other, with its stately indecent double-meaning, a piece of sheer writing down to the populace. In spite of these efforts to manufacture connections and of the closeness with which its plot follows on, *Henry V* is as truly separated from the two parts of *Henry IV* as *Richard II* is allied to them.

But I need not deal exhaustively with the play's shortcomings, when they have been set forth in such masterly fashion by Mark Van Doren in his *Shakespeare*. I will rather point out how conscientiously Shakespeare fulfilled his double obligation: to the chroniclers and to his public. If his muse failed to ascend the brightest heaven of invention at least it tried to pay the debts it owed below the sphere of the moon.

First, Shakespeare through the mouth of the Archbishop prolongs the chronicle story of Henry's sudden conversion:

> Never was such a sudden scholar made;
> Never came reformation in a flood
> With such a heady currance, scouring faults.
> For never Hydra-headed wilfulness
> So soon did lose his seat, and all at once,
> As in this king.

To suppose that Shakespeare meant the Archbishop here to be wrong, just as Poins had been wrong, about Henry's true character is to introduce a subtlety quite alien to the rest of the play. Shakespeare is submitting to the popular tradition of the chronicles and going back on his own earlier creation. Another legacy of the chronicle tradition, Henry's rejection of his old companions, had been done justice to in the previous play. Yet Shakespeare is careful to bring it in again when he makes Fluellen say,

> So also Harry Monmouth, being in his right wits and his good judgments, turned away the fat knight with the great-belly doublet.

With this rejection was coupled the election of grave counsellors and the heed Henry gave them. And here Shakespeare pays his debt in full, and once again at his own expense. His Prince Hal had been an eminently self-reliant and self-sufficient young man, one who would never accept the advice of others without subjecting it to the closest scrutiny. In the debate in I. 2 on the French war Henry is a different person. He hardly interposes much less argues. As a thinker he is quite passive, leaving the business to others. When these have pronounced their verdict, he accepts it without a word of comment but initiates action with

> Call in the messengers sent from the Dauphin.

The perfect courtier in whom intellect and activity was finely balanced has given way to the pure man of action, whose thinking is done for him by his counsellors. His subsequent pedestrian thoughtfulness when he argues with Bates and Williams is inconsistent alike with Prince Hal's brilliant intellect and with the narrow activity he shows both in the scene with his counsellors and his courtship of Katharine. Then the chroniclers (Polydore Vergil and Hall) tell us that Henry was able to learn wisdom by historical precedent. Shakespeare makes his Henry refer to the past history of his country:

> For you shall read that my great-grandfather
> Never went with his forces into France
> But that the Scot on his unfurnish'd kingdom
> Came pouring.

Finally, the chroniclers make much of Henry's piety, and Shakespeare follows them very conscientiously. He pays his debt; but at what a cost. We have only to compare Henry's pious comments on the miraculously low number of English casualties at Agincourt (twenty-five) and his orders for the *Non Nobis* and the *Te Deum* to be sung, with the last scenes of *Richard III* and certain parts of *Hamlet* to recognise how chilly they are. The platitudes of piety can become ultimate statements of overwhelming power if they issue from a worthy context. Occurring as they do here in a play which is constructed without intensity, they can only depress.

Other debts to the chroniclers concern not Henry's character but ideas about history. Before dealing with these I will speak of Shakespeare's fulfilling his debt to his audience by making Henry the hearty king, the good mixer. It was probably his sense of this debt that made him depress Henry's intellectual power in the debate about the French war referred to above. He fulfils it in Henry's familiarity with his "kinsman" Fluellen and his exchange of gages with Williams. But it is in his courtship of Katharine that Henry reaches his full degree of bluffness and heartiness. "I know not," says Johnson, "why Shakespeare now gives the king nearly such a character as he made him formerly ridicule in Percy." Johnson may well ask; for the whole distance between the poles divides the lubberly wooer with his coarse complexion, who "could lay on like a butcher," from the "king of courtesy" of the earlier play.

To revert to the chroniclers, Shakespeare does in *Henry V* keep alive the theme of civil war, but more faintly than in any other of his History Plays. He clearly intended the play to be a splendid interlude, when the ancestral curse was for the moment suspended, figuring in some sort the golden age of Elizabeth. But the curse is not forgotten, for Henry prays before Agincourt that the death of Richard II should not be visited on him then, and he even remembers it when he courts Katharine:

> Now, beshrew my father's ambition! he was thinking of civil wars when he got me: therefore was I created with a stubborn outside, with an aspect of iron.

And the conspiracy of Richard Earl of Cambridge actually re-enacts the theme.

In one historical matter *Henry V* is unique in Shakespeare: its partiality to things Welsh refers obliquely to that side of the Tudor myth . . . which Spenser and Warner, among the poets, developed.

> *Fluellen*. All the water in Wye cannot wash your majesty's Welsh plood out of your pody, I can tell you that. God pless it and preserve it, as long as it pleases his grace, and his majesty too!
>
> *Henry*. Thanks, good my countryman.

I fancy too that Shakespeare spares the French king the ridicule he heaps on the Dauphin, because he was father of Katharine, who, widowed of Henry V, married Owen Tudor and became the ancestress of Henry VII. The French king always speaks with dignity.

I wrote above that *Henry V* was constructed without intensity. It is worth mentioning one or two points in which this is true. After the Archbishop's fable of the bees there is little of the cosmic lore that marks the other History Plays. When Shakespeare's mind was working intensely it was aware of the whole range of the universe: events were not isolated but took place concurrently with other events on all the planes of existence. But the settings of the different scenes in this play are simple and confined. Even the battle of Agincourt evokes no correspondences in the heavens or elsewhere. A second sign of slack construction is the unevenness of the verse. There are passages of flatness among the rhetoric. The rhetoric has been better remembered than the flatness. But take the opening of II. 4 (the first scene showing the French court) up to the arrival of Exeter: it is written in the flattest verse, a relapse into the style of the more primitive parts of *1 Henry VI;* and, though Exeter proceeds to liven things a little, the verse remains lethargic. Nor is there much energy in the verse portions of the play's last scene. A third sign of weak construction is the casualness of the cosmic scenes. Whereas in *Henry IV* these were linked in all sorts of ways with the serious action, in *Henry V* they are mainly detached scenes introduced for mere variety. The farewell scene of Pistol and the Hostess in London is good enough in itself, but it is quite episodic. It would be unfair, however, not to mention the redeeming brilliance of Fluellen. For sheer original invention Shakespeare never made a better character. Had the rest of the play backed him up, he would (as his creator probably meant him to do) have filled the place of Falstaff not unworthily.

I fancy, too, that Fluellen helps us to understand Shakespeare's state of mind when he wrote *Henry V*. Fluellen is an entire innovation, like nobody else in Shakespeare before (though many years after he may have begotten the Baron of Bradwardine); and he suggests that Shakespeare was now wanting to do something fresh. Whenever Fluellen, the new character, is on the stage, Shakespeare's spirits seem to rise and he ceases to flog himself into wit or rhetoric. There are other things in the play that suggest Shakespeare's longing for a change. The coarseness of Henry's courtship of Katharine is curiously exaggerated; one can almost say hectic: as if Shakespeare took a perverse delight in writing up something he had begun to hate. Henry's reproof of Scroop, already noted as alien in tone to the norm of the play, has a quality as new as the character of Fluellen; for it is tragic and looks forward to Shakespeare's future bent of mind—

> May it be possible that foreign hire
> Could out of thee extract one spark of evil
> That might annoy my finger? 'tis so strange
> That, though the truth of it stands off as gross
> As black and white, my eye will scarcely see it.

That is one of the tragic themes: the unbelievable contradiction of appearance and reality; felt by Troilus about Cressida, by Hamlet about his mother, and by Othello about Desdemona. It has nothing to do with the matters that have most been the concern of this book: with politics, with patterns of history, with ancestral curses, with England's destiny and all the order of her society. It is a personal and not a public theme.

That Shakespeare was wanting to do something new is not at all to be wondered at. He had written his epic of England and had no more to say on the matter. In writing it he had developed characters of uncommon subtlety and in Prince Hal he had pictured a man, having indeed settled a conflict, but one in whom a genuine conflict had taken place. No wonder if Henry V, traditionally the man who knew exactly what he wanted and went for it with utter singleness of heart, was the very reverse of what Shakespeare was growing truly interested in. And no wonder if in his next great public character, Brutus, Shakespeare pictured a man like Prince Hal in being subjected to a conflict but unlike him in being torn asunder by its operations.

Shakespeare's Political Plays

by Una Ellis-Fermor

In the sequence of the history plays . . . we have primarily a group of four central plays supported by at least four or five more (one of which is of unquestioned dramatic power), extending together over several historical periods and introducing some two hundred different characters. This, of course, does not in itself guarantee the effect of vastness; it might merely guarantee chaos. But the balance and relating of characters in Shakespeare's hands are such that we experience the multifariousness of life and not mere confusion. The presence of some element of continuity between the plays of the main and even of the subsidiary group [1] is, I think, less obvious; but it is this which ultimately gives coherence to the wealth of material. In fact, it is pre-

[1] The group of plays with which we are mainly concerned here is the series *Richard II, Henry IV* (1 and 2) and *Henry V,* for in these four the simultaneous effect of epic space and dramatic concentration may be most clearly observed. But the gradually built-up figure of the kind, which gives significance and unity to this central group, is supported by the exploration and commentary of the four earlier plays, and by various studies of kings and statesmen in the later. Accordingly, I have sometimes drawn upon these also for their contributions, whether as a preliminary group whose significant order is that of the writing, or as subsequent observations and conclusions revealing the implications of the main group. There is a certain apparent inconsistency in deriving the union of epic magnitude and dramatic concentration partly from the earlier group of plays for which (with the exception of *Richard III*) we cannot claim the highest dramatic quality, and partly again from several detached later plays for which we cannot claim continuity of subject. But it is more apparent than actual; the contributions of the three earlier plays are almost entirely in the form of negative conclusions and the substance of their findings recapitulated in the main group, while those of the later plays are a revaluation of the central image of that same group. The service of both to the present argument is that of revealing explicitly what is included by implication in the main, and central, group, and thus permitting it to be stated more briefly and with fewer qualifications.

cisely here that the challenge of epic form to dramatic material arises. For a series of plays on related themes, with a certain number of overlapping characters, though clear and ordered in their individual disposal of their material, might yet remain no more than a number of excellent individual works of art, illuminating each other, but affording no continuous and coherent image, no central, emergent idea. Now, in most epic material we find a central figure, some aspect of whose life and experience forms a theme to which, should an epic poem be written upon that subject, everything in the poem could be made to contribute. Each character, episode, or group of events could bear, that is, a necessary relation to this central figure or idea, illuminating and illuminated by it, while at the same time maintaining its own relation, in the spatial and chronological scheme of the poem, with the other characters, episodes, and events. Aeneas's wanderings are a naturally shaped sequence, and can be causally related in a work of art, provided that all that is included affects or illuminates his experience and purpose.

This complete cohesion is characteristic only of the epic itself; there is, as a rule, only potential cohesion in the raw epic material. But is there anything akin to this potential continuity of epic material in the series of Shakespeare's political plays? Can we distinguish in them something which relates what would else be isolated units, causing them to illuminate each other and to contribute, each in turn, some indispensable part of a whole whose balance would be impaired without it?

I think we can distinguish some such factor in Shakespeare's series but . . . it will not be found in the generally prevailing mood of nationalism (and his attitude to nationalism passes through many phases between the writing of *Henry VI* and the writing of *Henry V*) nor in any single character. The central and continuous image in these plays, more specific than a mood, more comprehensive than a character, is, I believe, a composite figure—that of the statesman-king, the leader and public man, which Shakespeare builds up gradually through the series of the political plays from *Henry VI* to *Henry V*. This figure recurs, in varying forms, through the greater part of Shakespeare's drama, for after the picture is completed in the political plays he appears to revise and reconsider it, studying it from a different angle in several of the tragedies and late plays. For the purposes of this discussion we are concerned with the political plays, and chiefly with those four in which Shakespeare achieves simultaneously the abundance of epic material and the cogency of drama. But I have permitted myself, in order to indicate the vastness and complexity of this image, to include some evidence of his later thought; the revaluation, by reason of which he builds up a contrasting portrait, thereby making explicit and definite what had been implicit in that first portrait with which we are primarily concerned.

The portrait of the statesman-king is the result of a series of explorations, now the study of a failure, now of a partial success; a vast, closely articulated body of thought imaged always in terms of actual character, yet completely incorporated in no one character. The figure that finally emerges is not Falconbridge or Theseus or Henry IV or Henry V, yet it would be incomplete if any one of them were taken away; nor is it the mere opposite of Henry VI or John or Richard III or Richard II, yet it would also be incomplete if one of these were destroyed. These separate images are but statements or qualifications contributing to that vaster image, no one of them in itself coextensive with the composite whole. It is this which gives coherence to the material of the history plays, which nevertheless remain individual works of art. If it is true that Shakespeare has thus subdued potential epic material to dramatic form, may we now consider in more detail certain plays, in order to see how the emergent figure of the king dominates and draws to itself the whole of the central series?

Of the figures who appear in Shakespeare's political plays, we need survey only a certain group—the men upon whom the highest offices devolve. Inevitably, with an Elizabethan or Jacobean writer, this means the office of kingship, or of leadership in some form very like kingship. The position may be reached by violence and usurpation or by peaceful inheritance; in the first place the man may be capable of maintaining it and so partly justified in his action, or incapable of what he attempts, and so lose it; in the second case he may lend himself willingly to the task or it may be thrust upon an unwilling or an inadequate man. But in every case, from his earliest to his latest work, Shakespeare makes an imaginative exploration of the experience, adding something to the vast body of his comment on the figure of the statesman-king. Moreover, he is, broadly speaking, concerned in his Elizabethan phase mainly with what the office requires in the man, in his Jacobean phase with what the office does to the man. He passes, that is, from an interest centred chiefly in building up the picture of an ideal king or leader, to a study of the effect on the individual of the demands and privileges of his office.

Shakespeare's first explorations of this field seem to have been incidental to other work and to have led him, for the most part, to negative conclusions. The process by which he feels his way towards the centre of the experience is familiar to all his readers. The figure of Henry VI is the first which he is forced to consider (and at this early stage there presumably was an element of compulsion in the choice of the theme), and by his way of portraying the disasters of that reign Shakespeare shows clearly that he perceives some element of kingliness to be lacking. Henry is a pious, reflective man, by no means lacking in dignity, with a conscientious, but not necessarily intelligent, sense of his position. In an age when kings must be equally competent in peace and war, he is too simple for a politician (much less a statesman) and too ready to trust to conciliation to be a soldier. He lets his wife and his supporters fight his battle while he sits upon a hill alongside the field and laments that he had not been born a shepherd; yet at his death he claims in all good faith that he has loved his people and is convinced that they have no cause to desert him. A good man, a conscientious man, admirably suited for certain kinds of private, or, better still, monastic life; but neither firm, intelligent, shrewd, nor capable. A figure that tells us clearly that Shakespeare has already marked and inwardly digested the admonitions of the seventh chapter of Machiavelli's *Prince* and sees that ruthlessness is sometimes merciful and that a 'dangerous lenity' has no place among the 'king-becoming graces'.

Nor, for the matter of that, has a pure self-seeking individualism, and this type of leader he unhesitatingly despatches at the end of *Henry VI* and in the course of *Richard III*. What may be briefly termed the Tamburlaine–Hotspur–Essex–Byron figure that fascinated Chapman, the great lawless sixteenth-century nobleman whose purpose was his own glorification, had short shrift at Shakespeare's hands. Actually, Richard III receives less consideration as a type of leader than almost any other figure. He stands, in the group of Shakespeare's kings, as a crude but highly coloured specimen of the Tudor adventurer, storming his way to power, possessing the kingdom by violence, but unstable both on account of the violence of his passion and of some weakness inherent in the act of usurpation itself.

Indeed, it is this attitude of possessiveness that Shakespeare seems next to notice as one at least of the factors in the downfall of many leaders, and, as he defines it more clearly in *King John,* there forms behind it the shadowy suggestion of an opposite quality which comes, in the end, to be the essence of Shakespeare's positive ideal of kingship. The kings and rulers in *King John* all talk of their countries in terms of possession; the country is their property, they are landlords whose responsibilities go no further than treating it well enough to get a good yield from it; being men of sense, they preserve or protect it so that it does not depreciate, but there is no glimmer in their minds of any other feeling. Only in the mind of Salisbury, which misgives him at the thought of bringing civil war among the people he should protect, and in that of Falconbridge, who sees that the king is responsible for putting courage and good heart into his people, is there anything further. In Falconbridge we have a positive, if simple, ideal of service, a positive picture of kingly bearing and, incidentally, certain attributes that reappear in all Shakespeare's later successful kings; tenacity, resourcefulness, and shrewdness.

It is at this point that Shakespeare pauses to sum up, in a somewhat unexpected place, the positive findings of these first four political plays. The findings have, we admit, been up to now mainly negative—it is easier to write dramatically about disastrous reigns than about calm and prosperous ones, and there were more on record in the late sixteenth century. A king must not be submissive, conciliatory, and retiring (like Henry VI), however pious and conscientious; still less must he be a self-indulgent sentimentalist like Edward IV. But neither must he be a marauding egotist like Richard III, nor a landlord of his country like John, Philip, and the King of Austria. All these bring disaster with them and themselves end in disaster, because, however else they may differ, they are all at bottom individualists who have not sunk their individualism in their office of leader. It matters little to Shakespeare, at this stage and in this connexion, whether the individualism take the form of withdrawal from the world or of rapacious assault upon it, whether the natural habitat of the mind be a monastery or a battlefield. Both alike fail to meet the demands of sixteenth-century kingship because they do not think primarily of their office as a demand.

And it is here that the other figure to which I referred is interposed, that short study of a king who is indeed kingly; firm, just, even-tempered, possessed of a broad humanity and the characteristic Tudor love of his people, which, while it will no longer regard them as counters in an international gamble, yet knows precisely how to make a discreet display of that humanity and that love, so as to rivet unshakably the affections of those people. In the consciousness of the political value of these affections, no less than in the already slightly cynical realization of the manipulation needed to keep them at their height, Shakespeare has made a long step forward from the group of early historical plays.

> *The.* What are they that do play it?
> *Phil.* Hard-handed men, that work in Athens here,
> Which never labour'd in their minds till now;
> And now have toiled their unbreathed memories
> With this same play, against your nuptial.
> *The.* And we will hear it.
> . . . What poor duty cannot do, noble respect
> Takes it in might, not merit.
> Where I have come, great clerks have purposed
> To greet me with premeditated welcomes;
> Where I have seen them shiver and look pale,
> Make periods in the midst of sentences,
> Throttle their practis'd accent in their fears,
> And, in conclusion, dumbly have broke off,
> Not paying me a welcome. Trust me, sweet,
> Out of this silence yet I pick'd a welcome:
> And in the modesty of fearful duty
> I read as much as from the rattling tongue
> Of saucy and audacious eloquence.

This, it may well be contended, is not Theseus speaking, but, rather, a greater than Theseus, the last and greatest of the Tudor monarchs, who had 'the heart of a king and of a king of England, too'. But, what is equally significant for our purpose, it is already an anticipation of one of the dominant voices from the next group of plays, the group of the major histories, whose task is to build up the positive figure of kingship, to which the group of minor and preliminary histories have so far contributed only negative suggestions. The ground, then, has been thoroughly cleared by the time Shakespeare reaches the great tetralogy (*Richard II, Henry IV,* I and II, *Henry V*), and a few positive suggestions have been made.

The portrait of Richard II defines more clearly what is already implied, the fatal weakness of self-indulgent egotism, even though it be accompanied by private graces or virtues. But it adds, far more strongly, a picture of the fatal blindness that arrogates to itself the privileges of kingship while disregarding the responsibilities on whose account alone the privileges exist. Shakespeare's effective leaders, Falconbridge, Theseus, Henry IV, Henry V, Claudius, all see with perfect clearness the essential reciprocity of these two, and the last three at least have no sentimental illusions about either. Richard, in whom the sense of privilege amounts to megalomania, serves to define the extreme of that position, just as his immediate successor, Henry IV, defines the extreme position of the man oppressed by the sense of responsibility. (Here, as in so much else, it is Henry V who achieves the balance and reconciliation of the two.)

> Not all the water in the rough rude sea
> Can wash the balm from an anointed king;
> The breath of worldly men cannot depose
> The deputy elected by the Lord:
> For every man that *Bolingbroke* hath pressed,
> To lift shrewd steel against our golden crown,
> God for his *Richard* hath in heavenly pay
> A glorious angel. Then, if angels fight,
> Weak men must fail, for Heaven still guards the right.

But Richard, with his extravagant claims, serves a further purpose. His half-inspired, half-insane religiosity sees in the holder of his office the immediate representative of God on earth, claims for the king a consequent divinity, and genuinely believes that the hosts of Bolingbroke will fall before the 'glorious angels' whom 'God for his Richard hath in heavenly pay'. That there is something in what he says Shakespeare never, either at this time or before or after it, denies. In this particular play the very difficulty of dislodging Richard from the throne indicates it clearly, and in the earlier play we find that Henry VI is equally difficult to remove, while the courageous and astute Richard of Gloucester maintains his balance only with great difficulty and for a short time. There *is* something sacred in inheritance, and, though the evidence of the early plays has all pointed to the forming of this idea, it is in *Richard II* that, at a touch, it suddenly crystallizes out. Henry VI and Richard II, in their different ways inadequate men, have strong titles; and an unflawed title, if not half the king, is at least an important part of him. It is at least difficult to 'wash the balm from an anointed king' though it may not—and indeed does not—need 'all the water in the rough rude sea' to do it.

But if this hectic religiosity, this inflated claim of divine right, is fantastic in Richard's mouth, it is no longer fantastic when it haunts the broken dreams of the dying Henry IV. For the character and position of Henry IV introduce a set of problems the exact opposite of those of Richard II and new in Shakespeare's survey. Henry, fine statesman and excellent ruler as he is, is crippled and frustrated by his flawed title, and the sense of the sacredness of inheritance is as strong in him, who was perpetually reminded of his lack of it, as it ever was in Richard, and is accompanied by a far shrewder estimate of its significance.

The solution of the problems of the two parts of *Henry IV* and *Henry V* is the peculiar contribution of Shakespeare's Elizabethan phase to the summation of his idea of a king, of the man who should fit at every point the demands laid upon him by public office. Henry IV has all the qualities necessary to a king and avoids all the weaknesses of temperament in the portrayal of which the positive qualities have, so far, been implied. He has shrewdness, tenacity, and self-command that already approaches self-concealment; he has the true Tudor sense of the value of discreet popularity. He is as astute as a badger and has very much the same tough courage. He is not self-indulgent, he is not vain, he is not self-absorbed. He is not even a saint or a poet. He is an exceedingly able, hard-working statesman whose career reveals gradually but clearly the main qualification for kingship, the king's sense of responsibility to his people, that sense of service which, while making him no more than the state's greatest servant, makes all his privileges and exemptions, even a measure of autocracy itself, no more than necessary means for that service. Domineering he is, at times, like Shakespeare's prototype of Tudor monarchy, but he has, in the main, decent intentions, and he possesses, through thick and thin, an unfailing, humorous sense of proportion.

Having, then, such potentialities, why is he not the final figure in the group? The answer is obvious after the study of *Richard II*. The flaw in Henry's title, the fatal act of usurpation with which Richard had made such fine play, does indeed cripple his power and, through that, his mental stature, eating into his confidence and bringing down all loftiness of gesture or intention to the necessity of cunning and circumspection. Character no less than tenure suffers thus under the nemesis for an outrage done to the sacredness of inheritance. Henry IV is in nearly all things a potential Henry V and, trembling upon the verge of achievement, he looks into the promised land, and, as so often happens, speaks more explicitly of it than those who have dwelt in it familiarly. That is why it is, I think, impossible to understand Henry V as Shakespeare saw him, the Henry V who never speaks out, unless we can see his position and his intentions through the eyes of Bolingbroke's frustration:

> Heaven knows, my son,
> By what by-paths, and indirect, crook'd ways
> I met this crown: and I myself know well
> How troublesome it sat upon my head.
> To thee, it shall descend with better quiet,
> Better opinion, better confirmation:
> For all the soil of the achievement goes
> With me, into the earth.

It is left to Henry V to gather up in himself all that is fitting and necessary to a king and to remain as the epitome of the Elizabethan idea of the 'pollliticke vertues'. Shakespeare has at last resolved his demands upon such a figure into certain clearly defined qualifications and summed them all in Henry V, with his unflawed, hereditary title and his assured possession of all kingly attributes. With his broad-based popularity, his genuine love of public service for its own sake, his strong sense of responsibility, and his equally clear sense of its relation to privilege, his shrewd statesman's brain, successfully masked as that of a simple soldier, he stands where, perhaps, no king in drama has stood before or after him. Church and state, commoners and noblemen, soldiers and civilians, he knows them all, with a knowledge rooted in the taverns of Eastcheap, and holds them in his hand, too practised, popular, and secure to make a show of mastery. He was a statesman fulfilling Burke's demand—he knew how the whole world lived. He was a monarch, modelled upon the greatest of the Tudors, Elizabeth herself. It probably happens to every man to believe, at one time or another, for a time at least, that the greatest of the arts is conduct. And it is some such experience as this, in Shakespeare's career, that lies, I think, at the base of the great historical studies culminating in the figure of Henry V.

But if this were all, the composite figure would be shorn of half its subtlety and magnitude. We are aware already in this play that Shakespeare has gone beyond the experience he is primarily describing; that, implicit in this carefully balanced study, this culmination of so long and careful an exploration, is the germ of some later revulsion of thought which refutes it, as the great destructive speeches of Timon refute Ulysses' speech on the beauty of degree, of the ordered hierarchical state. For a while, it may be, between the writing of *Henry IV* and *Henry V,* Shakespeare believed the highest achievement of man to be the ordered state he afterwards described in *Troilus and Cressida,* the image of the ordered universe, of the cosmos with its regulated spheres.

> The Heavens themselves, the planets, and this centre,
> Observe degree, priority, and place,
> Insisture, course, proportion, season, form,
> Office, and custom, in all line of order: . . .
> But when the planets
> In evil mixture to disorder wander,
> What plagues, and what portents, what mutiny?
> What raging of the sea? Shaking of earth?
> Commotion in the winds, frights, changes, horrors,
> Divert and crack, rend and deracinate
> The unity and married calm of states
> Quite from their fixture? O, when degree is shak'd,
> (Which is the ladder to all high designs)
> The enterprise is sick. How could communities,
> Degrees in schools, and brotherhoods in cities,
> Peaceful commerce from dividable shores,
> The primogenitive and due of birth,

> Prerogative of age, crowns, sceptres, laurels,
> (But by degree) stand in authentic place?
> Take but degree away, untune that string,
> And hark what discord follows.

The keystone of this order was the figure of the perfect public man, of Henry V. All the implications of the foregoing plays point to this ultimate emergence of the complete figure. In all the anticipations that lead up to him, and particularly in the later scenes of the second part of *Henry IV,* Shakespeare has, he would seem to imply, 'in this rough work, shaped out a man'; the great art of conduct, and of public conduct at that, is at last truly understood.

But has he? Or has he, as it were unawares, and led already on to some perception beyond his immediate purpose, shaped out instead something that is at once more and less than a man. Henry V has indeed transformed himself into a public figure; the most forbidding thing about him is the completeness with which this has been done. He is solid and flawless. There is no attribute in him that is not part of this figure, no desire, no interest, no habit even that is not harmonized with it. He is never off the platform; even when, alone in a moment of weariness and of intense anxiety, he sees with absolute clearness the futility of privilege and the burden of responsibility, he still argues his case in general terms, a king's life weighed against a peasant's, peasant against king. No expression of personal desire escapes him; though he makes almost the same comparison as Henry VI, he is detached alike from king and shepherd, commenting upon them, but wasting no more strength on imagining what cannot be than on deluding himself, like Richard, with the empty glories of his state. He has inured himself so steadfastly to the life of a king, lived so long in councils and committees, weighing, sifting, deciding, commanding, that his brain automatically delivers a public speech where another man utters a cry of despair, of weariness or of prayer. It is in vain that we look for the personality of Henry behind the king; there is nothing else there. We know how his brain works upon any one of half a dozen problems; the treachery of Cambridge, Grey, and Scroop, the fomenting of wars abroad to preserve peace at home, the disaffection in the army, the difficulties of a formidable campaign, and the equally great dangers of a crushing victory. We see the diplomacy, the soldiership, the vigilant, astute eye upon the moods of people and barons, the excellent acting of a part in court and camp and council-room, and only when we try to look into the heart of the man do we find that it is hardly acting, after all, that the character has been converted whole to the uses of this function, the individual utterly eliminated, sublimated, if you will. There is no Henry, only a king.

I think Shakespeare was profoundly interested in this particular study. Not, indeed, by the character, for there is no character, but by the singular circumstances of its disappearance. Neither we the readers nor Henry himself nor his God ever meets the individual that had once underlain the outer crust that covers a Tudor monarch, for there is nothing beneath the crust; all has been converted into it; all desires, all impulses, all selfhood, all spirit. He is never alone, even with his God—least of all when he prays, for then he is more than ever in the council chamber driving an astute bargain, a piece of shrewd diplomacy, between one kind and another.

> O God of battles, steel my soldiers' hearts,
> Possess them not with fear. Take from them now
> The sense of reckoning, if th' opposed numbers
> Pluck their hearts from them. Not to-day, O Lord,
> O, not to-day, think not upon the fault
> My father made, in compassing the crown.
> I Richard's body have interred new,
> And on it have bestowed more contrite tears,
> Than from it issued forced drops of blood.
> Five hundred poor I have in yearly pay.
> Who twice a day their wither'd hands hold up
> Toward Heaven, to pardon blood. And I have built
> Two chantries, where the sad and solemn priests
> Sing still for Richard's soul. More will I do,
> Though all that I can do is nothing worth;
> Since that my penitence comes after all,
> Imploring pardon.

This king, as Shakespeare portrays him, is indeed 'a wondrous necessary man', the keystone upon which the sixteenth-century state depends, and individuality has at last been subjugated wholly to the demands of office. But it is not for nothing that generations of Shakespeare's readers have found little to love in this play. Unless we read it in the light of a certain bitter, underlying commentary, implicit in the orientation of the chief character, there is little there but that most grievous product of unremitting office, a dead man walking.

For the truth is that Shakespeare himself, now that he has built the figure with such care, out of the cumulative experience of eight plays, begins to recoil from it. It has been an experiment, an exploration, like, but for its larger scale, his brief but effective exploration of the system of Machiavelli, and, as he did with that system, so he does with this vast body of assembled evidence on public life: he rejects its findings as invalid before the deeper demands of the less explicit but immutable laws of man's spirit.

So much, then, for the Elizabethan phase of Shakespeare's portrait of the statesman-king, for the record of the period when he for a time believed that the wide canvas of public life was greater than the illimitable experience of the spirit. The contrast between the private and public virtues has been made clear, the qualifications of the great statesman have been slowly selected, tested, and built up into a single figure. Such characteristics as did not contribute to his public self have been eliminated (and they are seen, somewhat surprisingly, to be nearly co-terminous with character). More than this, certain of the loyalties, decencies, and ideals most prized in an individual are found to be incompatible with the public virtues. Henry, who rejected Falstaff in circumstances which cannot be forgiven, will also, in the moment of crisis, bargain with his God like a pedlar. His religion and his love for his people alike carry with them a tinge of expediency, a hint of the glib platform speaker.

It would seem, then, that in the very act of completing the figure, Shakespeare became aware of a certain insufficiency, and that dissatisfaction was already implicit in his treatment of Henry V, the culminating study of the series. What was there implicit is revealed by degrees in his treatment in the later plays of similar characters, or characters similarly placed. At the risk of straying a little from the immediate content of this discussion, may we consider Shakespeare's final comments? For the additional significance they lend to the earlier figure makes it yet more comprehensive because of the latent subtlety, the implicit qualification that they bring to light in it.

Now, in the very play which concluded his Elizabethan picture, Shakespeare indicates already the tone and direction of his Jacobean commentary, which is at first merely dissatisfaction and disillusionment. In the course of the corollaries added in the Jacobean period it becomes clear that the disillusionment follows his perception of the true nature of Henry's supreme achievement, the whole and integral subordination of his individuality to the office of leadership. Shakespeare never again gives us a full picture of a successful ruler, with the exception of the figure of Claudius (the somewhat cynical implications of this selection constitute a study in themselves) and for the most part the men who fail, in the Jacobean plays, to meet the demands of public life are of interest not because they prove unfit for office, but because they are unfitted by office for something which Shakespeare increasingly perceives to be of deeper value.

Henry the Fifth

by Derek Traversi

The national unity aimed at by Henry IV is finally achieved, in the last play of the series, by his son. The principal theme of *Henry V,* already approached in its predecessors, is the establishment in England of an order based on consecrated authority and crowned successfully by action against France. The conditions of this order are, again in accordance with the main conception, moral as well as political. The crime of regicide which had stood between Bolingbroke and the attainment of peace no longer hangs over Henry V—unless as a disturbing memory—and the crusading purpose which had run as an unfulfilled aspiration through the father's life is replaced by the reality, at once brilliant and ruthless, of the son's victorious campaign.

This, as critics have not always realized, is less a conclusion than a point of departure for the understanding of *Henry V.* It was the conditions of kingship, as much as its results, that interested Shakespeare in these plays; and these conditions are viewed, by the time the last of them came to be conceived, in a light definitely akin to the tragic. The problem of political unity and that of personal order have been brought in the course of these historical studies into the closest relationship. Just as the state, already in *Henry IV,* Part II, is regarded in its divisions as a diseased body ravaged by a consuming fever, so is the individual seen increasingly as torn between the violence of his passions and the direction of reason; and just as the remedy to political anarchy lies in unquestioned allegiance to an authority divinely constituted, so does personal coherence depend upon the submission

"Henry the Fifth," by Derek Traversi. From Shakespeare From Richard II to Henry V *(Stanford: Stanford University Press, 1957), pp. 166, 187-198.* *The first three sections of this chapter have been omitted.*

to reason of our uncontrolled desires. The link between the two states, political and personal, is provided in these plays by concentration upon the figure of the king. The problem of the state becomes, in a very real sense, that of the individual at its head. The king, who rightly demands unquestioning allegiance from his subjects, is first called upon to show, through the perfection of his self-control, a complete and selfless devotion to his office. The personal implications, as well as the military triumphs, which that devotion brings with it, are considered in *Henry V*.

* * *

IV

The scene which follows immediately on the elaborate set piece which constitutes the Prologue to the fourth act gathers up into an immediate form much of the truly personal feeling of this play. It will be clear by now that *Henry V* represents, however tentatively and partially and however mingled with other purposes related to the original chronicle conception, a step in the realization of themes only fully developed in the tragedies. Inheriting a conception of Henry as the victorious ruler, perfectly aware of his responsibilities and religiously devoted to the idea of duty, Shakespeare seems to emphasize the difficulties of the conception, the obstacles, both personal and political, which lie between it and fulfilment. These difficulties, however, never amount to a questioning of the royal judgement. Even in his decisive debate with Williams and Bates on the morning of Agincourt (IV. i), where the implications of his power are most searchingly discussed, the king's right to command obedience is never in question. The claims of authority, as fundamental to the Shakespearean conception of the body politic as are those of judgement and control to the moral idea, must still be advanced and accepted. Henry's soldiers, in spite of their pessimistic views of the military situation, accept them without reserve. For Bates the duty of a subject lies in loyal execution of the royal will, and the responsibility for wrong action, if wrong there be, rests beyond the simple soldier with the king: 'we know enough, if we know we are the king's subjects.' Williams is more sceptical, but his scepticism, far from sapping the will to action, as it might have done in the following 'problem' plays, reflects a sturdy and independent nature. Replying to Henry's assertion that the cause is just with a doubtful 'that's more than we know,' he never questions the postulate that the subject is bound to obey. On the contrary, he openly asserts that this is so. To disobey, as he puts it, 'were against all property of subjection,' and the emphasis is still upon the 'proportion' to be observed between king and subject, directing head and executing body, and upon the proper submission required for the successful military effort. Henry, of course, accepts this view of his position. Indeed, the temper of the play, still strongly orthodox in its politics, would not in any case permit him to do otherwise; but the manner of his acceptance, modified as it is by a consistently sombre estimate of human possibilities, is at this moment decidedly tragic in spirit.

For the arguments of his followers, though they do not—and cannot—lead Henry to question his own authority, correspond to his own mood, force him to reflect deeply upon the weaknesses which even kings cannot overcome. It is in the tone of these reflections that he approaches most closely the spirit of later plays. 'The king is but a man, as I am: the violet smells to him as it doth to me; . . . all his senses have but human conditions: his ceremonies laid by, in his nakedness he appears but a man; and though his affections are higher mounted than ours, yet when they stoop, they stoop with the like wing.' There is about the argument a universality which transcends the royal situation. Men, differentiated by a 'ceremony' ultimately vain, are united in their common 'weakness,' and the most notable feature of human behaviour seems to the speaker to be its domination by impulse, its helplessness before the universal stooping of the affections.[1] In this respect, at least, the king is one with his men; and just because he is so like them, because his senses too 'have but human conditions' and are continually liable to break through the guard of rigid self-control imposed upon him by his vocation, there is something precarious and disproportionate in his absolute claim upon the

[1] The reference to the violet and its smell in connection with corrupt sensuality can be paralleled in the words of Angelo in *Measure for Measure,* II. ii:

It is I
That, lying by the violet in the sun,
Do as the carrion does, not as the flower,
Corrupt with virtuous season.

allegiance of his followers. Nowhere in this play are we closer to the spirit which, modifying the simplicity of the original conception, carries us forward in anticipation of the tragedies to follow.

The tragic spirit is expressed through the king's increasing awareness of his isolation. Williams underlines this when he points out the spiritual consequences of a conflict for which his master, as unquestioned head of his army, is alone responsible: 'For how can they [Henry's soldiers] charitably dispose of any thing, when blood is their argument? Now, if these men do not die well, it will be a black matter for the king that led them to it.' These words repeat once more, but with a greater urgency, the preoccupation with the horrors of war which Henry has already expressed, even if he succeeded in shaking off responsibility for them, to the French ambassadors and to the Governor of Harfleur. They repeat it, moreover, in terms of that friction between flesh and spirit, the presence of which is so persistently implied in the king himself. The words of Williams indicate, in fact, beyond the religious sense of responsibility which derives from the traditional conception of monarchy, a contrast—already familiar—between the Christian law of 'grace' or 'charity' and the 'blood'-spurred impulse to destruction that threatens it in the necessary acts of war with the consequences of unleashed brutality. The connection between this conflict of flesh and spirit and the tendency of human societies, states, and families alike to dissolve by the questioning of 'degree' into anarchy is not established in this play as it is in the tragedies which follow. But Hamlet himself might have reflected like Henry on the precarious basis of human pretensions, and Angelo defined in similar terms the catastrophic realization of it brought about by his fatal encounter with Isabella. Had Henry once followed his line of speculation far enough to doubt the validity of his motives for action, or—on the other hand—had he given free play to the sinister impulses he dimly recognizes in himself, the resemblance would have been complete; as it is, there is only a premonition, a first indication of possibilities brought more fully to light in later plays.

For the moment, Henry counters Williams' argument by pointing out that soldiers 'purpose not their death, when they purpose their services.' The latter's sombre view of human nature, however, imposes itself upon the king, attaches itself to his own meditations, and is profoundly echoed in his words. Connecting war with sin, and in particular with overriding passion, he repeats the tone of earlier statements: 'Besides, there is no king, be his cause never so spotless, if it come to the arbitrement of swords, can try it out with all unspotted soldiers: some peradventure have on them the guilt of premeditated and contrived murder; some, of beguiling virgins with the broken seals of perjury.' The result is, in part, a fresh emphasis on meticulous self-examination as a means of conserving spiritual health—'Therefore should every soldier in the wars do as every sick man in his bed, wash every mote out of his conscience'—and, in the verse soliloquy which closes the scene, one of those outbursts of nostalgic craving for release which have appeared already in *Henry IV*, Part II, and will be repeated with a new, more *physical* apprehension of existence in Hamlet's soliloquies and the Duke's incitations to Claudio in *Measure for Measure:*

What infinite heart's-ease
Must kings neglect, that private men enjoy!

The craving for 'heart's-ease' in this long speech is still, generally speaking, what it is in *Henry IV*—a desire to be freed from the burden of an office in which human purposes seem so often fatally divorced from human achievement. The development of the verse is still painstaking, leisurely in the expansion of its long periods, and a little rhetorical; but there are moments, generally traceable to characteristic touches of imagery, which anticipate the association in *Hamlet* of this familiar nostalgia with a desire to be free from the intolerable incumbrances, the 'fardels,' the 'things rank and gross in nature,' by which the flesh persistently seems to obstruct the unimpeded workings of the spirit. 'Greatness' is a 'fiery fever' which consumes its royal victim like a bodily disease, and the contrasted peace of the humble subject is described with a curious ambiguity of tone:

Not all these, laid in bed majestical,
Can sleep so soundly as the wretched slave,
Who with a body fill'd and vacant mind
Gets him to rest, cramm'd with distressful bread.

(IV, i)

In the association of peace with bodily fulness and vacancy of mind, in the impression, harshly and directly physical, behind 'fill'd' and 'cramm'd,' there is a distinct suggestion of certain descriptions of satiated, idle contentment in plays as far apart as *Troilus and Cressida* and *Coriolanus.*[2] Here already such imagery represents a kind of residue standing, intractable and irradicable, in direct contrast to the king's increasing emphasis on the need for spiritual discipline. It is no more than a suggestion, unabsorbed as yet into the main imaginative design of the play; but, tentative as it is, it stands in a certain relationship to the clash of flesh and spirit—'passion' and 'grace'—which exacts continual vigilance from Henry, and which is slowly moving through these developments of imagery towards more open realization.

The tragic sense which dominates this episode is finally related, before it concludes, to a main argument of the entire series, the sense of the crime, still imperfectly expiated, by which Henry's father took possession of the crown, and which still lives at this moment of self-scrutiny in his own mind:

> Not to-day, O Lord,
> O, not to-day, think not upon the fault
> My father made in compassing the crown! (IV, i)

In this reflection, at least, the religious note which runs through Henry's utterances is associated with a sense of deeper feeling than elsewhere; and by the end of the same speech, after he has listed his efforts at reparation, the sense of being unable to escape the consequences of past actions emerges with an intensity that anticipates the presentation of some of the great tragic figures:

> More will I do;
> Though all that I can do is nothing worth,
> Since that my penitence comes after all,
> Imploring pardon. (IV, i)

The expression here, though not of course the speaker's situation, recalls that of Claudius in his vain attempts to pray.[3] The later Shakespearean villains—Claudius and Macbeth—seek to repent, but are unwilling to relinquish the fruits of their original crime. Henry's situation, it need hardly be said, is not the same as theirs. The most hostile

[2] I have indicated the importance of imagery of the same type in both these plays in the sections devoted to them in my book *An Approach to Shakespeare* (Garden City, N.Y.: Doubleday & Company, Inc., 1956).

[3] *Hamlet,* III. iii.

interpretation could not make him in any sense a 'villain,' and the 'crime' committed to which he refers is not his but part of the burden planted upon him and carried to Agincourt; but in the expression, at least, there is sufficient similarity to indicate that one of the themes which were later to bear fuller tragic expression is here in the process of emerging from a play conceived originally in a very different spirit.

V

After this introduction, the scenes leading up to and including the battle of Agincourt strike us, in the main, as belonging rather to the chronicle material than to the more deeply personal conception of the play. The first two (IV. ii and iii) set forth once more the contrast between the spirit that animates respectively the French and English camps. The French are introduced (IV. ii) with the spurious lyricism that has throughout been characteristic of them. Orleans refers at the very start to the sun that gilds his armour, and he and the Dauphin go on to apostrophize, in French, the elements as indicative of their conquering spirit. The object of this presentation, however, is rather plain ridicule than any contribution to the spirit which prevails in the better scenes of the play; when the Constable goes on to speak in contrast of the 'starved band' of English as 'shales and husks of men,' his account is connected, poetically speaking, with the spirit of the Prologue to this same act and stresses, dramatically, the folly and vanity of the estimate so lightly delivered. The following account of the English put into the mouth of Grandpré is still more clearly a piece of literary elaboration, laboured in its pictorial emphasis and charged with a weight of descriptive content that gives to such phrases as 'The gum down-roping from their pale-dead eyes' a sense of artificiality which fails to contribute, by mature Shakespearean standards, to any living effect. We may feel in these lines the effort of the literary craftsman to extend and define his style through recourse to a conscious artifice perhaps not entirely disconnected with the more elaborately wrought verse of certain parts of *Troilus and Cressida,* but less related to any discernible unity of spirit.

In contrast with this vacant and pretentious verbalism the English, regarded so mistakenly as 'lifeless' by the French (whose conception of 'life' has just been proved, rather heavily, to be so artificial and without content), are presented (IV. iii) in a scene in which the patriotic purpose of the original history prevails almost exclusively. A sober confidence and piety is the keynote to the scene, and from it the king's own set-piece of rhetoric, in the 'Crispin Crispian' speech, emerges naturally as the thing it is—an admirable piece of declamation based on values which the most mature part of Shakespeare's experience, in the very act of accepting them, was already subjecting to a disturbing contact with other, more complex ways of thinking. The Shakespeare who put into Henry's mouth the words,

> if it be a sin to covet honour,
> I am the most offending soul alive,

would appear, at first sight, not to be the one who had already, in Falstaff's repeated utterances, exposed to examination the same concept of 'honour' and arrived, on some occasions, at very different conclusions. He is clearly a less complex and, in some sense, a less interesting writer; and yet we should not understand the full achievement of the mature dramatist if we did not see that this too is an essential element that went to the making of it. If Falstaff, at his best moments, rejects a certain conception of 'honour,' he does so in the name of life, of a vitality that will not be constrained to the empty forms of rhetoric which interest manoeuvres for its own ends; and if the clash between this refusal and a positive attitude which is not less necessary for its deliberate dedication to the public, the political sphere, produces—in the later plays of the sequence—an outlook increasingly sombre, the simple acceptance of duty is still a possible, and indeed necessary attitude. Henry is never more attractive than at this moment of accepted decision, when his dedication to the responsibilities of office blossoms forth into a simple and deeply human comradeship.

Only at the end of the scene, when the French herald comes to demand ransom, does the king's anger express itself in something like the iron rigidity we have learnt to associate with him in earlier scenes. The reference to the 'dead bodies' of the coming battle—who are to be famous,

> for there the sun shall greet them,
> And draw their honours reeking up to heaven;

Leaving their earthly parts to choke your clime,
The smell whereof shall breed a plague in France
(IV, iii)

—some critics will perhaps be content to relate to the spirit of the times; but the note struck is not dissimilar to one we have learnt to associate with Henry from the time of the attack on Harfleur. It belongs, indeed, to his nature, and—we may say, without overstressing the point—to the less admirable part of it, which always emerges when his will is crossed or his self-esteem insulted; and it is not until we return to the sober note of

tell the constable
We are but warriors for the working-day,

that the more positive conception again prevails.

The battle scenes which immediately follow scarcely add to the stature of the play, though one or two touches contribute to the complete conception. The first (IV. iv) could be regarded as a comic commentary, offered through the bragging of Pistol, upon the heroic conception of war; and yet its content forbids us to claim so much individuality for it. It is worth reflecting that the original titles advertising this play recommended Pistol as its chief comic attraction: worth remembering because that is in itself some comment on the change of mood since the rejection of Falstaff.[4] The chief quality of Pistol is *emptiness,* a bombastic show that wordily covers vacancy: as the Boy, whose remarks throughout are a kind of dim shadow of the comic perspicacity of his former master, puts it, 'I did never know so full a voice issue from so empty a heart.' Pistol is *empty,* indeed, both of sense and of the comedy that goes with it. The most significant phrases uttered by this camp follower, this scavenger of fortune, are those which turn upon the theme of throat-cutting, already anticipated by Nym[5] and to be echoed again in the scenes immediately following. The Boy, turning from him, contributes to the spirit of the whole when, after comparing Nym and Bardolph favourably to 'this roaring devil i' the old play,' he goes on to refer to them as *dead,* eliminated by the ruthless—and necessary—moral efficiency on which Henry's victory is to be built. 'They are both hanged': the times have changed indeed, and the empty

[4] Reference here is to the title page of the Quarto edition.
[5] See [II. i.]

brags of Pistol are hollow echoes of a comedy that has ceased, since Falstaff died, to illuminate events with its own distinctive life.

The short intervening scene (IV. v) in which the French, having failed in manliness and efficiency alike, rush to their fate, calls for no comment. The next (IV. vi) is only remarkable for the romantic deaths of Suffolk and York, steeped in gore and in the familiar imagery which, from the time of the earlier chronicle plays on the reign of Henry VI, associates love and death:

> over Suffolk's neck
> He threw his wounded arm and kiss'd his lips;
> And so espoused to death, with blood he seal'd
> A testament of noble-ending love.
> The *pretty* and *sweet* manner of it forced
> These waters from me which I would have stopp'd.

Poetic effects similar to these, deriving from Shakespeare's early manner, appear in his later work in connection with a firmer and more dramatic grasp of the realities of character; but here, as the final adjectives show, the romantic and decorative elements prevail in a thoroughly theatrical comradeship in death. The scene ends, however, on a grimmer note in Henry's concluding command to 'every soldier' to kill his prisoners. The juxtaposition with the preceding heroics, though we need not go so far as to imply a condemnation foreign to the spirit of the times, cannot be altogether accidental.

The throat-cutting note, indeed, is carried on, in the next scene (IV. vii) to the end of the battle. It is a necessary part of Henry's triumph. Justified as it no doubt is in terms of military tactics, it is also related to the tougher strain of disillusioned realism that emerges from the play. The self-control which we have learnt to associate with the victorious king is, as we have repeatedly had occasion to see, not without a suggestion of harshness and inhumanity. His righteousness is of the kind that does not prevent him from inflicting merciless reprisals on his enemies, reprisals preceded by the characteristic rising of a passionate anger—

> I was not angry since I came to France
> Until this instant

—which the justice of its occasion does not make less typical of the speaker's nature. This anger, once it has taken possession of him, expresses itself in the cold purposeful determination that has always been part of his make-up:

> Besides, we'll cut the throats of those we have,
> And not a man of them that we shall take
> Shall taste our mercy. (IV, vii)

This is once more the Henry who can contemplate suffering from which his normal, peaceful humanity would recoil, but of which he feels himself, in war, not to be the cause. It is, moreover, an action for which much in the so-called comic action has prepared us,[6] and which leads us to find something sardonic in Gower's comment that 'the king, *most worthily,* hath caused every soldier to cut his prisoner's throat. O 'tis a gallant king!' By such excellence, Shakespeare would seem to say, must wars be won.

The rest of this episode adds little of interest to the play. The final count of the dead on either side, and Henry's dedication of his 'miraculous' victory to the will of God, related though they are to his character as consistently developed, belong to the spirit of the original chronicle; and the comic business between Williams and Fluellen, arising out of the king's earlier discussion with the former, reflects not the spirit of comedy associated with the prose scenes of the preceding plays, but the sense of tough loyalty which is closer to the new conception and belongs—in its better moments—to the ultimately tragic tendency which the play reveals. The best of this scene is contained in Fluellen's expression of devotion to his king: 'I will confess it to all the 'orld: I need not to be ashamed of your majesty, praised be God, *so long as your majesty is an honest man.'* [7] Should we need a word to describe the best positive values of this play, that which distinguishes it from mere patriotic rhetoric on the one side and sardonic pessimism on the other (and both moods are constituent parts of it), it would be the word 'honesty' as here used; honesty which can offer loyalty whilst maintaining independence of judgement, and which is brought out, as much as the cruelty which balances it, by the sombre circumstances of war which no merely patriotic show of rhetoric or romantic comradeship in death can conceal. This 'honesty,' expressed also by Williams in his robust self-defence before Henry—'you ap-

[6] See the relevant phrases of Nym, Macmorris, and others.
[7] *Henry V,* IV, vii.

peared to me but as a common man; . . . and what your highness suffered under that shape, I beseech you to take it for your own fault and not mine'—is characteristic, in its directness, of the play. These soldiers, revering the necessary form of monarchy upon which all social order depends, can yet see in it the reflection of their common humanity. It is this reflection, by which they are ennobled, which has brought them to victory over enemies for whom 'common' humanity is no object of reverence or understanding. If this understanding points eventually to an intuition increasingly tragic in its implications, it is also related to the patriotic purposes which equally prevail in this play.

By the time we reach the opening of the last act, we are in a position to understand why *Henry V* has been most generally popular when imperfectly understood. The concessions made to human feeling in some of the most individual parts of the play are too few, their presiding spirit too rigid, to compel enthusiasm. It ends, as far as the supposedly 'comic' action is concerned, in a decided pessimism which somehow fails to attain the note of tragedy. Pistol, speaking the last word for the cutthroats of the play, leaves us, after Gower's condemnation of him as 'a counterfeit cowardly knave,' [8] with a gloomy and realistic vision of his future which the sober common sense of his companions does not sufficiently lighten:

> Doth Fortune play the huswife with me now?
> News have I, that my Nell is dead i' the spital
> Of malady of France;
> And there my rendezvous is quite cut off.
> Old I do wax; and from my weary limbs
> Honour is cudgelled. Well, bawd I'll turn,
> And something lean to cutpurse of quick hand.
> To England will I steal, and there I'll steal:
> And patches will I get unto these cudgell'd scars,
> And swear I got them in the Gallia wars. (V, i)

The reference to Nell's death and the nature of it are alike significant. They stress, like so much in this play, the passing of the comic spirit so strongly revealed in its predecessors, and relate that passing in terms which look forward to the disillusioned realism of the 'problem' plays.

[8] *Henry V*, V. i.

Pistol is the last and least worthy survivor of another world, and his anticipated future looks forward to a very different one to come.

Nor is the political conclusion, which shows peace following on the English triumph, much more encouraging. Burgundy's picture of the benefits of peace and the destruction of war is couched in the decorative vein which we have found elsewhere in what we have called the chronicle matter of this play. True in itself, as far as it goes, its sense is rather public than personal, and its tone makes no pretence to intimacy. The marriage project itself belongs to this order of reality. Katharine of France is, after all, part of the spoils of war; and if Henry woos her with direct simplicity, he has none the less his political purpose clearly and constantly in mind. It is characteristic of him that when he turns to the king of France and asks him to ratify the match—'Shall Kate be my wife?'—his comment when he has received the reply 'So please you,' links his acceptance to the extension of his territorial power: 'I am content; *so the maiden cities you talk of may wait on her:* so that the maid that stood in the way for my wish shall show me *the way to my will.*' [9] It is Henry's virtue, as it is also his limitation, to live entirely, exclusively for the public function which he has accepted as his vocation; and it is therefore fitting that the marriage with which he rounds off his victory is primarily an act of policy.

The nearest approach to a moment of true feeling is that in which the king, in his characteristic, direct prose, contrasts the passing nature of man's decorative virtues with the constancy of 'a good heart':

> a speaker is but a prater; a rhyme is but a ballad. A good leg will fall; a straight back will stoop; a black beard will turn white; a curled pate will grow bald; a fair face will wither; a full eye will wax hollow: but a good heart, Kate, is the sun and the moon; or rather the sun and not the moon; for it shines bright and never changes, but keeps his course truly.
>
> (V, ii)

This, at least, belongs rather to Henry's virtues than to the political arrangement being proposed. The same virtues enabled him, on the morning of Agincourt, to unite his followers in the true fellowship of 'a band of brothers.' They are no mean virtues, but that they are mainly dedicated to the public, the political sphere is never more clearly shown than in the manner of this wooing. Henry's approach

[9] *Henry V,* V. ii.

to Katharine, with its plain and dispassionate honesty, befits what is after all a political agreement undertaken finally in a spirit of sober calculation. It may have satisfied the demands of patriotic orthodoxy at Elizabeth's court; but Shakespeare had the gift of fulfilling obligations of this kind without being deterred from his deeper purposes, and this conclusion, while it confirms Henry's characteristic virtues, limits firmly the range of emotions which he is capable of feeling. Not to have limited them, indeed, would have been to create a figure humanly more interesting but, for that very reason, politically less effective. The inspiration of *Henry V* is, in its deeper moments (which do not represent the whole play), critical, analytic, exploratory. As we follow it, and in spite of our admiration for its hero's dedication to his chosen ends, a certain coldness takes possession of us as it took possession, step by step, of the limbs of the dying Falstaff; and we too, as we come to the end of this balanced, sober study of political virtue rewarded by the success it deserves, find ourselves in our own way 'babbling of green fields.' [10]

[10] Theobald's famous emendation has, of course, its difficulties; but in the absence of an alternative which shall appeal both to sense and the poetic instinct we may perhaps be allowed to retain it.

Ambivalence: The Dialectic of the Histories

by A. P. Rossiter

. . . These kings and great persons are all sub-tragic. They lack a degree (or some degrees) of freedom; are caught in nets of events by which they are frustrate and less than their potential selves. In Rilke's phrase, they are *Verwirrt mit Wirklichkeit:* bondsmen to a 'reality which is that of the world of action, therefore temporary, pragmatic, unreal. And they (to quote Yeats again):

> Constrained, arraigned, baffled, bent and unbent
> By those wire-jointed jaws and limbs of wood,
> Themselves obedient,
> Knowing not evil and good;
> Obedient to some hidden magical breath.
> (*The Double Vision of Michael Robartes*)

The mechanism to which they are subjected is that process of 'retributive reaction' which is the only *tragic* component of the Histories.

Retributive Reaction is my name for the principle of the simplest of the patterns in these plays; of which pattern we see only a short and misleading section in the Richard-to-Henry V tetralogy. There, the usurpation of Bolingbroke (exactly described in terms of consequences by Carlisle), with Richard's death by murder, leads on to the Unquiet Time of Henry IV—to the Percies' Rebellion, and the father's fears that Prince Hal is just another Richard; and so up to the death-scene in 'Jerusalem' and 'God knows, my son . . .' followed by the advice to 'busy giddy minds/With foreign quarrels': which is—despite

"Ambivalence: The Dialectic of the Histories," by A. P. Rossiter. From Talking of Shakespeare, *ed. John Garrett (London: Hodder & Stoughton, Ltd.). Reprinted by permission of Hodder & Stoughton, Ltd., and Max Reinhardt, Ltd., London.*

all that Archbishops may say—the political reason for Henry V's French campaign. That is victorious, and the curse of usurpation seems to sleep. Yes, to *sleep;* it is not dead.

The closing chorus of Henry V refers back to the Henry VI series, the loss of France—'which oft our stage hath shown'. Thus the sequel to *Henry V,* in the complete pattern, is 'Hung be the Heavens with black' and the Roses series, where 'civil dissension' carries forward the curse of royal murder, uncertain or divided right, brother against brother, for the sixty years to Bosworth Field.

. . . Taken all together, the Histories are a dark glass, where we gaze *per speculum in enigmate.* The mystery beneath the surface of the magic mirror with its shows of kings is chill and deeply saddening.

> Action is transitory; a step, a blow,
> The motion of a muscle, this way or that,
> 'Tis done, and in the after-vacancy
> We wonder at ourselves like men betrayed;
> Suffering is permanent, obscure and dark,
> And shares the nature of Infinity.
>
> (Wordsworth: *The Borderers*)

. . . On Order, Degree, and so on, let me be brief: the essentials only need recall; let me remind you:

The State, as monarchy, is ordained by God; its structure is hierarchical, and in health all its orders or degrees are 'congreeing in a full and natural close/Like music' (as Exeter says in *Henry V,* I. ii). To all orders as way of life there is 'fixed as an aim or butt/Obedience' —as the Archbishop goes on to say, using bees as ideals or exempla. (The whole speech is very serious; whatever Stratford producers may choose to do with comic clergymen.) From the principle of Obedience —which really means a complete system of proper respects towards all superiors from parents upwards—it follows that the rightful King is, as it were, the organic nucleus of the cell-State; and that without due and rightful succession all Order (all its vital processes) is put in jeopardy. The only right way with a bad King is non-resistance: biding God's good time in Christian patience—as Gaunt tells the wronged Duchess of Gloucester—for ill Kings are as much ordained by God as good ones.

The curse of usurpation is that it confuses Right, endangers all

Order. That of rebellion is that it commits the Luciferian sin of pride, and destroys all Order: by the assumed 'law' that men who will revolt against the highest loyalty (to God's Deputy) cannot be bound by any other loyalty, nor decency. The rebel abrogates all respects; and since the King-enucleated State is ordained by God, by Natural Law, therefore he is a thing *unnatural:* a boil, a plague-sore, a carbuncle of corrupted blood.

. . . I can do no more but only remark in passing how irony—including 'dramatic irony'—is a display of an essential ambivalence. Dramatic irony causes an exact juxtaposition of opposites in the mind of the audience: opposites, in that the 'true' for one hearer (the stage Persona) must exclude the 'true' for other hearers, who take the same words in a far extended sense, of which the hearing Persona is known to be unaware. ('Fail not our feast', e.g.) Yet both meanings only happen in the same mind: the audience's or reader's. The emotive effect is a terrifying belittlement of human prescience or judgement, as in tragedy, when we project the simple meaning on to the mind of a Macbeth, then contemplate it, as it were, against the ironized, unsimple meaning. Or, where sympathy lacks, the effect is some kind of detached sardonic amusement: as in some of Richard III's ironies, or, perhaps, in watching Falstaff and Co. scampering up to London for Harry's coronation, with Shallow in tow and all to the tune of: 'Let us take any man's horses. The laws of England are at my commandment. Happy are they which have been my friends; and woe unto my Lord Chief Justice.'

We have seen the Prince reconciled to the L.C.J.—we know the rest. But though this is still irony, it is now Comic Irony: in which pathos, derision, a sad wry smile and a malicious grin strive together—and all 'belong'. A modern Mirror-for-Magistrates view, to which Falstaff is only the 'Vice' to be formally discarded in a moral interlude of princely education, leaves just nothing of all that doubleness of feeling.

But Shakespearian History plays double tunes on far more than the comic aspects of the misfortunes of an old fat cynical reprobate—even when they do (as here) symbolize the absurd vanity of human wishings (which supply all beggars with dream-horses at the twinkle of a main-chance). Consider how in both parts of *Henry IV* the shady and seamy sides of glorious War are presented; and comically. In Part 1

Falstaff explains how he damnably misuses the King's press (IV. ii.). In Part 2 a full-length exposition of the game is given (III. ii.), with Feeble as the unwittingly ironical commentator—laughed at for a fool, yet the only man's-size voice in Gloucestershire:

> By my troth, I care not; a man can die but once; we owe God a death. I'll ne'er bear a base mind. An't be my destiny, so; an't be not, so. No man's too good to serve's Prince . . .

The Mug is the Hero, without prejudice to his mug-dom: the Fool is the only clear-seer. Ambivalence again. And all comic; though implicitly all these 'King's press' episodes are serious commentary on the wickedness and irresponsibility inseparable from WAR. Damnably wrong, clean contrary to all the war-values associated with Crécy, Agincourt or Harfleur . . . and *therefore* a critical comic commentary on a set of human facts which the 'Agincourt-values' insist on viewing (if at all) with one eye only. 'Two voices are there', as Wordsworth said in quite another connection: 'This is damnably wicked', says the one. 'It's damn' funny', says the other. Historian Shakespeare heard both.

I shall not labour to explain how the famous 'Honour' catechism comically balances the accounts of that main term in *1 Henry IV;* but I must remark on the beautifully complicated parallelisms generated when Falstaff tells the Prince how his father has sent for him, and that he had best rehearse before he goes to the palace to explain himself. It is a scene which travesty-parallels the true meeting later (III. ii), and it is Eastcheap interlude-acting played to the height.

First, KING Falstaff rebukes his 'son' (with a parody of Puritan oratory), allowing that he *has* observed *one* virtuous man in Harry's company: 'If that man should be lewdly given, he deceiveth me; for, Harry, I see virtue in his looks.' Next, the Prince insists that they change roles, and we have the Prince (as King) pretending just what he will *have* to pretend when he *is* King: viz. that Falstaff is 'an old white-bearded Satan', a 'villainous misleader of youth'. The picture is the obverse of Falstaff's; but now Shakespeare goes one better still, and makes Falstaff as Prince offer a final turn of defence—ending with 'Banish not him thy Harry's company. . . . Banish plump Jack, and banish all the world.' To which the King-Prince replies—as the Prince-King will have to in earnest—'I do, I will'.

In that three-move epitome you have all the special technique of the *Henry IV* plays: a constant shifting of appearances, like the changing lights of an opal, so that every event, every person becomes equivocal—as Falstaff made Honour. That Gadshill robbery is not mere farce. If we 'realize' it, in an Usurper's state where Henry's right is only that of might, might only—then what are the Percies and Bolingbrokes but Gadshills, Bardolphs, Petos in Bigger Business?

> Thieves for their robbery have authority
> When judges steal themselves

so says Isabella in *Measure for Measure.* The comic robbing of the robbers is comically parallel to what the King would do with Percy's Scots prisoners; and the difficulty of establishing the Right in anything, in an England under no rightful king, is paralleled and parodied throughout in Falstaff's 'manner of wrenching the true cause the false way'—whether in the inventive proliferation of buckram men, in belying Mrs. Quickly to the Lord Chief Justice, or bamboozling her into vigorous denials of her own (perhaps not impeccable) virtue. I mean where he calls her an otter, and explains 'She's neither fish nor flesh; a man knows not where to have her.' To which the wronged woman replies in great moral indignation, 'Thou art an unjust man in saying so. Thou or any man knows where to have me, thou knave thou.'

It is in all such places—in Falstaff as the Wit: the witty equivocator who turns all to mirth, destroying ideals and seriousnesses with a turn of the word—that the Comic Histories go beyond anything that Shakespeare attempted in *Richard II.* There, too, that the narrowly Tudor-political or 'moral' approach will most oversimplify, and thin, the true Shakespearian vintage. The 'moral-historical' approach diminishes Falstaff as Wit, leaving him with little more than the rascally quick-wittedness which gets Eulenspiegels and Harlequins out of tight corners. Sir John is more. He is not only witty in himself (No, I'm not going on with Familiar Quotations)—he is Wit ipse. And wit is critically destructive—of ideal systems which assume that human nature is what it isn't. The doubleness of implicit values in those situations which are ambivalent; those which can be seen as serious *and* farcical: as pathetic *and* absurd: as abominable *and* laughable: as fine-and-admirable *and* as all-very-fine-and-large; all that centres on Falstaff. To read it as simply 'evil' (or 'the antithesis of the Princely virtues') and to make 'evil' the opposite of the Order required by the military State of a Henry V, is too naïve. And I don't mean just 'too naïve for 1951', I mean 'Too naïve for the mind of a Shakespeare, in 1599'. As Walter Raleigh wrote:

> This is indeed the everlasting difficulty of Shakespeare criticism, that the critics are so much more moral than Shakespeare himself, and so much less experienced. . . . The ready judgments which are often passed on Shakespeare's most difficult characters are like the talk of children. Childhood is amazingly moral, with a confident, dictatorial, unflinching morality. The work of experience . . . is to undermine this early pedantry . . . to teach tolerance, or at least suspense of judgment.

That's a 'period-piece', no doubt, and I wouldn't endorse its rather shapeless liberalism, which half suggests the (to me absurd) conclusion that Shakespeare is not moral at all—let alone one of the greatest of moralists. But Raleigh didn't have the word 'doctrinaire' to hand, I suppose. The warning he gives is by no means out of date, I should say.

I hope I'm not slipping towards (what he would call) the surprising moral immaturity of some of our doctrinaire contemporaries,[1] if I say that there is, in Falstaffian wit, something of the devaluating skill of The Devil. Let me hide behind Coleridge to advance my point. In table-talking on 16 February 1833, Coleridge gave a long account of a Faust play he had designed before ever he read Goethe. (I don't believe him, but that's unimportant.) He said, 'My Devil was to be, like Goethe's, the Universal Humorist, who should make all things vain and nothing worth, by a perpetual collation of the Great with the

[1] An instance I may have had in mind in 1951 will be found in Mr. D. A. Traversi's study of *1 Henry IV* in *Scrutiny* XV. I. pp. 24 f. Having fixed 'moral' prejudices from the start, Traversi damns Douglas with a supreme moral confidence, ascribing his own notions to the Prince. Thus: "when he describes him he stresses the same lack of imagination . . . later found in the Greek heroes of *Troilus and Cressida*. Douglas is the man who "kills me six or seven dozen of Scots at a breakfast" and then complains of "this quiet life," the man who is not above filling out his prowess in battle with unimaginative boasting &c.' (p. 27). Later we find, 'Douglas is as the Prince has described him a brainless butcher . . .' (p. 31: the rest continuing the Wilson Knight formula from *Troilus and Cressida* in *The Wheel of Fire*). Traversi never sees that his quotation is about *Hotspur,* nor that Scotticide is improbable in a Douglas. School-children produce just such fantasy-figures, with similarly misapplied quotations. *Sed quis custodit* [*? scrutinat*] *ipsos Scrutineres?*

Little in the presence of the Infinite.' Now surely that is very near to what Falstaff does, when most the Clown critical. 'The perpetual collation of the Great with the Little' is no bad formula for what Shakespeare is repeatedly doing in both *Henry IV* plays.

In Part 2, however, the Universal Humorist is a far more sardonic one than before. Not only in that Old Age, in its failings, its brags, its pavidities and follies, is a major theme; nor only that Lord John of Lancaster's 'victory' is disgracefully won; there is more besides. To hint that 'more', I'll glance at the very first speech: '*Enter Rumour painted full of tongues*'.

> Open your ears; for which of you will stop
> The vent of hearing when loud Rumour speaks?
> I, from the orient to the drooping west,
> Making the wind my post-horse, still unfold
> The acts commenced on this ball of earth.
> Upon my tongues continual slanders ride,
> The which in every language I pronounce,
> Stuffing the ears of men with false reports.
> I speak of peace while covert enmity,
> Under the smile of safety, wounds the world;
> And who but Rumour, who but only I,
> Make fearful musters and prepared defence,
> While the big year, swoln with some other grief,
> Is thought with child by the stern tyrant war,
> And no such matter? Rumour is a pipe
> Blown by surmises, jealousies, conjectures,
> And of so easy and so plain a stop
> That the blunt monster with uncounted heads,
> The still-discordant wavering multitude,
> Can play upon it. But what need I thus
> My well-known body to anatomize
> Among my household? Why is Rumour here?

That is the first part of the speech. It is followed by a list of the tales which are spreading from the Battle of Shrewsbury, and the piece concludes thus:

> The posts come tiring on,
> And not a man of them brings other news
> Than they have learnt of me. From Rumour's tongues
> They bring smooth comforts false, worse than true wrongs.

Rumour's prologue offers a theme which runs right through the whole play; a theme which invites a sardonic, detached, unsympathetic or coldly-critical attitude towards all the agents in the historic field. *False-report befools everyone.* Not only in the rumoured rebel victory at Shrewsbury; not only in the false (favourable) report of Falstaff's prowess—to which Coleville surrenders, and which even the L.C.J. makes some allowance for. Falstaff's own trust in the Prince and his star is also 'smooth comforts false': as is old Shallow's trust in Sir John and the smell of Court. So too—false—is this same Shallow's roaring-boy Past in London. And Pistol is false-alarm personified: mouthfuls of Theatre masquerading as a man—whereas he is nothing but wind. And thus the parallel to 'Sir John to all Europe': the vain delusion to which Coleville surrenders, as the northern rebels surrender to 'smooth comforts false' from Westmorland and Prince John. Finally, the King—King Hal the First—that Falstaff expected to find in London is only a delusion; and the laugh is on Falstaff—with a grating edge to the amusement. (A. C. Bradley only encountered this unhappy Mixed Feeling at the Rejection. In fact it starts much earlier in the play. Modern 'moral' critics apparently never meet it at all.)

These shifting mirage-like effects of unstable appearances relate Part 2 to the so-called 'Problem Plays' (which *I* call 'Tragi-comedies'). They develop from, e.g., the Honour theme of Part 1, but go well beyond that historical Comedy.

And if you wonder why—talking on 'The Histories'—I say so little about *Richard II* and *Henry V*, my answer is: I am diagnosing their shortcomings by focusing attention on Shakespearian History at its highest development. (I say 'History'. If you want to see this kind of thing taken on, in later work, go to the Galley-scene in *Antony and Cleopatra:* a similar comedy, sardonic comedy, of the frailty of the Great: the strange absurd chances that turn the fate of worlds.) But in *Richard II*—either Shakespeare was bent on following Marlowe and writing an unEnglish tragedy (i.e. without comic interplay: though *Woodstock* put it directly before him); or he knew instinctively that the preciosity and self-regarding sentiment of Richard *could not stand* comic criticism or even lapse of seriousness.

In *Henry V* his aim was changed. Whatever he once intended (and that last speech, by the Dancer, in *2 Henry IV,* does show the *intention* to export Falstaff to France), what he produced was a propaganda-play on National Unity: heavily orchestrated for the brass. The sounding—and very impressive—Rhetoric shows how something is being stifled. The wartime-values demand a determined 'one-eyedness'; the King fails to reach the fullest humanity because of that demand. He *has* banished Plump Jack;. and 'all the World' has been banished with him. At least, the 'Allness' is gone. The play is 'fracted and corroborate'.

Without going all the way with 'Q', to say that Falstaff must go to 'Arthur's bosom' because he can kill Harry with a look, I do agree that Sir John had to be dead; for fear of the damage he must needs have done by babbling of (not 'green fields') . . . by killing the heroics with a jest. When the ranks are closed, and to question is to lack Will, to falter, then there is not so much freedom of mind as will say *outright* what every sane man knows (however brave): 'I like not such grinning Honour as Sir Walter hath. . . . Give me Life, say I.'

There are fine things in *Henry V;* but much of the comedy has lost touch with the serious matter. It's a play Shakespeare had finished with well before he finished it. His falling-back on the old *Famous Victories* for that slapdash stuff—treating the Princess of France like a Free Frenchwoman, etc.—that shows it. It surprises me that our London dramatic critics should have been surprised to find that as a climax to the 1951 Stratford historical tetralogy it does not come off. The truth is, the heart of Shakespeare's insight into English History (which means a good deal more than the History of England)—the *heart* is in the middle of the sequence: in the *Henry IV* plays, where he turned back from the sentimental seriousness of *Richard II*, back to the kind of Comic History he had made rough beginnings with in Parts 2 and 3 of *Henry VI*. (Where he had achieved something remarkable in the grotesque, Hieronymus-Bosch-like sarcastically-comic scenes of Cade's rebellion.) [2]

To see why *comic* History was his true genre, it is needless to go

[2] I mean such Bosch paintings as *Ecce Homo* and the Veronica picture, where the mob is not only grotesque—absurd and half-diabolic—but also presents itself as a kind of hydra: *belua capitum multorum;* cf. Rumour's 'the blunt monster with uncounted heads', etc. The phrase was a commonplace, unoriginal even in Horace's day; but Bosch actualizes it in paint, as Shakespeare does in drama. A European tradition is shared by the Flemish painters and Shakespeare. I explored a fringe of it in an article on *Breugel's Ambivalences* in *The Cambridge Journal* for December 1948.

back to the evolution of the Elizabethan Drama and its Miracle-play and Morality-play underlays. 'Mungrell tragy-comedy' *was* the mere-English genre, but never mind that now. Look only at *King John*—those lines by the Bastard on 'Commodity' ('Mad world, mad kings . . . etc.')—and you will see how they take the gilded lid off the lofty illusions of theoretical Tudor Politics (I mean *Stage*-politics). By-passing all the ideals of Order, Degree, Non-resistance, Right-divine and God's-deputyship, the Bastard exposed the world of politics as 'a racket'.[3] The thought implicit in the making of that speech has the same quality of deep political penetration that emerges from the conflict of serious and comic in *Henry IV*—and in *Coriolanus* and *Antony and Cleopatra*. That speech shows the same ambivalence, but simpler; for Falconbridge is a noble fighting humorist as well as a critical wit. He is not, like Falstaff, a Universal Humorist; but some of the undermining intellectual clearsightedness of the later Histories is there.

Throughout the Histories it is in the implications of the Comic that shrewd, realistic thinking about men in politics—in office—in war—in plot—is exposed: realistic apprehension outrunning the medieval frame. Because the Tudor myth system of Order, Degree, etc. was too rigid, too black-and-white, too doctrinaire and narrowly moral for Shakespeare's mind: it falsified his fuller experience of men. Consequently, while employing it as FRAME, he had to undermine it, to qualify it with equivocations: to vex its applications with sly or subtle ambiguities: to cast doubts on its ultimate human validity, even in situations where its principles seemed most completely applicable. His intuition told him it was *morally* inadequate.

Hence the unhappy feelings which generous-minded critics have displayed about the Rejection of Falstaff. That some of them have *overdone* it is neither here nor there. It is well enough for Dr. Tillyard or Professor Dover Wilson to tell us that the Prince *had* to cast off Sir John. We know that. We know what Kingship meant to textbook Tudors (far better than the Globe audiences knew, I dare say). Yet I still feel that as Shakespeare *was* Shakespeare—the man who made

[3] This was put too crudely. I would add now: Shakespeare wrote in an unstable equilibrium between a 'World' or 'Universe-of-thought' of faith in God-ordainedness, and another World: the Inverted World of belief only in Power. The 'Inverted World' symbol is familiar in Breugel's pictures, as an orb with its cross downwards. The 'upsidedownness' notion is in *Measure for Measure* and elsewhere. The pictorial emblem itself appears in Quarles (e.g. *Emblems* i. 15).

Hermione and Hamlet, drew Kate Percy as war-widow (a traitor's wife by the Code), drew Katherine as the fallen majesty of England—he must have known, *and felt,* the lack of humanity (of generosity, high-mindedness, true magnanimity) in his Hal in that scene. And again, I think, in Henry's treatment of the conspirators at Southampton; where the King is so obviously playing a publicity propaganda part, as Justice, iron-visaged, pitiless. . . . As obviously as he said he was in that first of unprincely soliloquies, 'I know you all. . . .' (*1 Henry IV,* I. ii. end.)

Is there not a resemblant quality in his father: the 'silent king', Bolingbroke, in the mirror-episode in *Richard II?* A separateness from the feeling world, which makes the actor in public affairs assume a predetermined part, like a *play*-actor, only with all his directives outside and none of his? One of those 'who, moving others, are themselves as stone', as the sonnet phrases it: 'the lords and owners of their faces'? And thus again a resemblant quality in John of Lancaster's treachery to the northern rebels? Oh, I know it can be argued that, to the Elizabethans, no ill treatment or trickery towards rebels could be unjustified. But can we assume that Shakespeare's sensibilities were so crass as not to know meanness as meanness, perfidy as perfidy, when it could be said to have profited the State? I say no more than, 'I think not'. And if you agree on any of these points I've hung on to the Rejection of Falstaff, doesn't it follow that you are made to *feel* (not merely 'see', notionally) how the frame of Order, the coherent rigid medieval system accepted by some of our most reputed modern scholars, is outrun by that mind which Jonson (who 'knew the man . . . etc.') considered to be 'not for an age but for all time'?

It follows, if I have taken you along with me, that we cannot dissect-out, stain and fix the system of Shakespeare's reflexion on History. A rigid political-moral good-and-evil system is there; but as the events and the people speak into our inner mind, we find that Shakespeare is shifting subtly from key to key, as if by what musicians call 'enharmonic changes': using ambiguous note-sequences till contradiction is itself confounded, and yields a precise evocation of the paradox of human experience.

Thomas Mann has explored this musical symbolism to the limit in his vast, amazing, fascinatingly wearisome novel *Doktor Faustus.* When his damned musical genius, Adrian Leverkühn, makes his first experiments with notes, the narrator (Serenus Zeitblom Ph.D.) records a comment which seems to be saying a lot about what I find in the ambivalences of Shakespeare. 'Relationship is everything', said Leverkühn. 'And if you want to give it a more precise name, it is Ambiguity . . .' And again, later, 'You know what I find?—That music turns the equivocal into a system' (pp. 47 f. of the American translation approved by Mann. Knopf, 1947).

What is more, Leverkühn finds something amenable to his music in Shakespeare. He takes *Love's Labour's Lost* as a theme to treat. On this Zeitblom reports, 'He spoke with enthusiasm of the theme, which gave opportunity to set the lout and the 'natural' alongside the comic sublime, and make both ridiculous in each other.' Mann is not explicit, but it is clear enough that he means the three lover-nobles by 'comic sublime', placed *vis-à-vis* Costard as 'the natural'. Zeitblom Ph.D. is unhappy about it: 'I have always been rather unhappy at the mockery of humanistic extravagances; it ends by making Humanism itself a subject for mirth' (p. 164). That would be a good text for setting out to explore the entire subject of so-called 'Comic Relief' in Shakespeare. I must keep within my limits, come back to Histories.

'Music turns the equivocal into a system.' That is why I used the phrase 'The Dialectic of the Histories' in my—admittedly alarming—title (for which I now apologize). The Order-code-system of Tudor theory approaches History with the kind of argument that Plato called *eristic:* that is, argument aimed at the extinction of an opposite and 'bad' system of beliefs. The code is moral, but in the narrow sense: too much so for Shakespeare's contemplation of mankind; too narrow and bounded for his human insight, from which he derived a *political wisdom.* As Hazlitt once observed:

> Shakespeare was in one sense the least moral of all writers; for morality (commonly so called) is made up of antipathies; and his talent consisted in sympathy with human nature in all its shapes, degrees, depressions and elevations.

I shan't examine that for its shortcomings, beyond saying that it is *morally* acuter than Raleigh—as witness the distinction 'morality commonly so called'. Taking it as it stands, then, I say: Therefore, Shakespeare's intuitive way of thinking about History (which we cannot formulate as an abstracted notional system) is *dialectical.* The old eristic-argumentative system which he used is static, changeless; but *his* thought is dynamic, alterative, not tied to its age. It has that extra degree-of-freedom which is given only by what I called a constant 'Doubleness': a thoroughly English empiricism which recognizes the coextancy and juxtaposition of opposites, without submitting to urges (philosophical, moral, etc.) to obliterate or annihilate the one in the theoretic interests of the other. That is what I tried to express by the figure of 'two-eyedness'.

His awareness of the 'soul of goodness in things evil' is not less than his sense of the spirit of seriousness (or significance) in things base—or foolish—or farcical—or indecent. To laugh at Hotspurious honour is as good as to think. To laugh at Shallow, or at Falstaff with Doll Tearsheet, is the substance of some wry or wringing thinking. But no less funny for that. And thus it is that the serio-comic dialectic of the Histories leads on to the Tragedies, where you have (as in the Histories you have not, I consider) Coleridge's 'collation of the Great and the Little *in the presence of the Infinite*'. In none of the Tragedies is the Order-system the friend of human greatness; rather the enemy.

If you have difficulty in refusing the critics' directions to see Henry V as Shakespeare's Ideal; if you cannot quite accept what I've said about the constant Doubleness of the Shakespearian vision in the Histories; then let me ask you to face a straight question: 'WHO, in the later, greater plays, are the heirs and successors of those Order-symbols Henry V and Henry Tudor (the triumphant Richmond of the end of *Richard III*)? The men who are, to the State-order system, 'goods': unifying nuclei of the organism, whether a People or the mind itself: the beings on whom the political heaven smiles. Who are they?' I should reply, 'The Fortinbrasses, the Octavii, Lodovicos, Macduffs, the Edgars and Albanies. On whose heroic qualities Bradley is, for once, entirely adequate.'

But why is 'the other side', the reverse to the kingly, historic, patriotic obverse, the Comic? Is it not partly this? In History Shakespeare felt that men were constrained to be much less than their full selves. He knew the burden of princehood: the Ceremony lines alone would proclaim it. All the Lancasters are less than full men. None is himself; only what he wills to be for the time only. By and by he will 'be more himself'. Hal says it: Father says it. None does it. Richard does try to be himself, full kingly length. He finds a shadow in a mirror.

Only the other Richard—Gloucester—can say, 'I am myself alone'. And *he* is the Devil, spinning the orb on his thumb. Now Comedy is the field of human shortcoming; and therefore Shakespeare's History, at its greatest, *had* to be comic. What isn't Comic History in the Histories is what I can only call 'Obscure tragedy'.

Henry V

by M. M. Reese

. . . After the sustained conflicts of the two preceding plays, *Henry V* is in the main a demonstration. The hero is no longer in the toils. The end has proved the man, and his victory over himself has been much more than a personal victory. Riot and dishonour have been put to flight, reason is passion's master, and England has at last a king who can physic all her ills. Because he has proved himself a valiant and chivalrous prince, and one who acknowledges the sovereignty of law and justice, the crown comes to him 'with better quiet, better opinion, better confirmation', and all the soil of the Lancastrian achievement has gone with his father to the grave. In *Henry V* Shakespeare celebrates England's recovered majesty through the deeds of 'the mirror of all Christian kings'.

A formidable body of critical opinion is hostile to this view. In general it is held that, if this really was what Shakespeare was trying to do, he failed to bring it off; his natural scepticism could not help revealing the essential hollowness of this idealised and unlikely figure. Obviously there is something in this. Shakespeare was much too conscious of the human pressures that weigh on a public man to believe that a whole reign—even a short one that enjoyed God's special care—could be conducted on this rarefied level, and he has allowed the human material to be transformed by the universalising tendencies of epic. But the hostile critics have various kinds of objection to the play. They are united only in their dislike of Henry, and they find different ways of rationalising their prejudice. Purely subjective notions paralyse their judgment, and they write as pacifists, republicans, anti-clericals, little Englanders, moralists, even as arbiters of etiquette, until one is astounded at the prejudice Henry has managed to arouse. In all the canon only Isabella, in *Measure for Measure,* has stirred so much personal distaste. In the meantime all contact is lost with Shakespeare's purpose and achievement. Dr. Johnson wrote of the play without much enthusiasm, but at least he noted (with reference to Shakespeare's endless enjoyment of the joke about the warming properties of Bardolph's nose) that 'this poet is always more careful about the present than the future, about his audience than his readers'. The immediate effect in the theatre was what concerned him most.

Hazlitt went full-tilt at the play, branding Agincourt as a royal Gadshill and describing the Archbishop of Canterbury as a pander to riot beside whom Falstaff was only 'a puny prompter'. Henry made war on his neighbours because his own crown was doubtful and he did not know how to govern the country anyway. Hazlitt concedes that 'we like him in the play. There he is a very amiable monster, a very splendid pageant', to be admired rather as one gazes at a caged panther in the zoo. But objective criticism of the play was made impossible by the writer's Francophil republicanism. He admired Napoleon but not 'this star of England'. A hundred years later Mr. John Masefield, in not dissimilar terms, found in Henry 'the knack of life that fits human beings for whatever is animal is human affairs': a back-handed compliment at the best, but almost the only one he is willing to pay to a man whom he reckoned to be 'commonplace'. Bradley, who could not stomach the rejection of Falstaff, allowed Henry a certain coarse efficiency but thought him to be inescapably his father's son, 'the son of the man whom Hotspur called "a vile politician".' The key to the reign is therefore to be found at *2 Henry IV* IV v 176–218; and presumably there is not much point in reading *Henry V* at all. Granville-Barker found the play to be lacking in any 'spiritually significant idea': which is patently absurd, since in Shakespeare's time the wise government of states was one of the highest destinies to which God might call a man. But Chambers says much the same thing: 'Here you have a Shakespeare playing on the surface of life, much occupied with externalities and the idols of the forum. And with the exception of a few unconsidered words that fall from the mouth of a woman of no reputation, there is nothing that is intimate, nothing that touches the depths.'

More recently, and more soberly, Dr. Tillyard has given Shakespeare credit for good intentions but concludes that he set himself an impossible task. Shakespeare's Hal, so warm and human, was irreconcilable with the copy-book hero of popular tradition; and Tillyard blames the sources for the fact that the king is a lesser person than the chivalrous prince who won Vernon's heart (*1 Henry IV* IV i 97–110). Mr. Traversi finds human flaws in Henry's total self-dedication to the business of being a king, and, like Bradley, he feels the father's influence to be still pervasive. The coldly official manner masks a personal inadequacy of which Shakespeare was evidently aware.[1]

There is no means of persuading people to like Henry if they lack the inclination, but at least we should recognise what Shakespeare was trying to do and how he set about it. Popular legend gave him a paragon, as Tillyard says. It was sufficiently potent to cause Polydore Vergil to break off his mainly critical narrative and insert a most uncharacteristic eulogy. Hall, Daniel, Drayton and Raleigh all came under Henry's spell, Hall in particular finding him the cradle of all the royal virtues: 'a king whose life was immaculate and his living without spot . . . a shepherd whom his flock loved and lovingly obeyed . . . he was merciful to offenders, charitable to the needy, indifferent to all men, faithful to his friends, and fierce to his enemies, toward God most devout, toward the world moderate, and to his realm a very father'. This was Shakespeare's feeling about him too; and it is important to remember that he did not accept the legend without examining it. In two plays devoted to the education of a prince he built up Henry's character so that men could believe in it, showing the human weaknesses as well as the dedication and conveying the magnitude of the responsibility by hinting at the personal sacrifices which it demanded. He does not allow us to think of Henry as an angel temporarily borrowed from above. The character gains its strength and conviction from all that has gone before, not from *Henry IV* only but from all the poet's earlier studies of kingship and society. In these studies he has shown us not only the sort of man the ideal king will be but also the roots from which he must grow; good government re-

[1] W. Hazlitt, *Characters of Shakespeare's Plays;* J. Masefield, *Shakespeare;* A. Bradley, *Oxford Lectures on Poetry;* H. Granville-Barker, *From 'Henry V' to 'Hamlet';* E. K. Chambers, *Shakespeare: a Survey;* E. M. W. Tillyard, *Shakespeare's History Plays;* D. A. Traversi, *Shakespeare from 'Richard II' to 'Henry V'.*

sults from a complex of social and moral relationships, and *Henry V* is a play about England as well as about a single heroic man.

Is it a successful play? The proof is in the theatre; and critics who dislike the play may fairly be asked to give an honest answer to the question of what their response has been when—if they ever have—they have seen it acted on the stage. No play of Shakespeare's has such a simple, unvarying effect. It is absolutely proof against the perversity of directors. It is quite impossible to do anything 'clever' with it, and the only way of producing it is the way the author indicated long ago. Nor does it fail in its impact. In times of war and national danger men have been inspired by it; but even at ordinary times, when one perhaps goes to the theatre in no mood to be stirred by elementary heroics, the play's energy and its uncomplicated sentiment unite the audience in common surrender. In the theatre it is no longer possible to have any doubts about Henry himself. If Shakespeare had any secret reservations about the character, they are not apparent on the stage, where Henry is virtuous, strong and gay, a born leader of men. It is quite evident that Shakespeare approves of him; just as, in his own dramatic terms, he approves of Isabella and does not approve of Shylock.

Of course the play's appeal and interest are limited, and this very limitation makes its unfailing success in the theatre the more remarkable. Technically it is a considerable achievement, since Shakespeare was writing in a mode that he recognised (and he admits it often enough) to be extremely difficult.[2] 'O for a Muse of fire.' He decided that the noble deeds of Henry V, which were of a kind to inspire wonder and imitation, could not be fittingly celebrated except through the medium of epic; and epic and drama are not naturally congenial to one another. The well-known admissions in the Prologue are not just an apology for the theatre's failure to accommodate marching armies: Shakespeare was quite ready to stage a battle when it suited him, and with no apology for the small numbers engaged in it. The Chorus was a device that he seldom used, and never so extensively as in *Henry V*. Its function here is to apologise for the unsuitability of any stage for the breadth and sweep of epic; but at the same time Shakespeare

[2] Cf. the judgment of J. H. Walter in the introduction to the new Arden edition, p. xvi: '*Henry V* is daringly novel, nothing quite like it had been seen on the stage before.'

uses it with great boldness and ingenuity to make good some of the deficiencies he so modestly admits. He tells the story of the reign in a sequence of episodes, linking them by speeches in which the Chorus supplies gaps in the narrative and generally sets the mood for the following scene. This is a practical function of some value, as we can discover from those episodic chronicle-plays where no such assistance is supplied. But the verse of the choruses, corresponding to the passages of heightened description which a narrative poet habitually employs, has the further function of establishing the epic stature of the hero.

Properly the hero's qualities should be established through the dramatic action, and the prominence of the Chorus, like the element of rhetorical strain often detectable in the verse, is a weakness that necessarily results from the use of the epic mode: Shakespeare was trying to do something that did not wholly belong to drama. His method was to illuminate his hero in a succession of facets. Dover Wilson calls them tableaux,[3] and they may be compared with magnificent stained-glass windows whose panels unfold a story. But tableaux and stained-glass windows do not move. Their nature is to crystallise an emotion, and it is a just criticism, so far as it goes, that the ritualistic style of the play confines the hero to certain rigid, one-dimensional attitudes. Henry's character is immediately established in the opening conversation between the two ecclesiastics, and it does not develop thereafter. Nor, despite the immense surface energy which keeps the play moving in the theatre,[4] is there any real conflict. Henry has risen above temptation, and there is nothing to excite us in his calm pursuit of an assured destiny. Doubts assail him only twice, when his bedfellow betrays him and when ordinary soldiers question the justice of his war. But even then—so it is said—the official manner does not relax. He always seems to be speaking 'for the record', and even in soliloquy he addresses himself as though he were a public meeting.

The familiar criticisms start from here. Henry is smug and hypocriti-

[3] In the introduction to his Cambridge edition, xii.

[4] On the lower levels, obviously, the play was composed with great technical assurance. There is conflict of a kind in the clashes between the English and the French both at court and on the battlefield; the two camps are excellently contrasted, and Shakespeare has found room for a rich variety of character and incident, all of it related to the central theme.

cal; or he exists only on the surface and is simply too good to be true. Then it is only a short step to more serious accusations, and Henry's behaviour is condemned by standards not in the least applicable to his time and state. It is easy to see how this has happened. Epic praises heroes and denounces villainy. It does not deal in light and shade, and its blacks and whites have a definition too simple for the give-and-take of ordinary life. Aeneas is always *pius,* Odysseus always πολύμητις, because the poet does not mean to complicate the fundamental issues. So with Henry: if in the play his virtues seem to be superhuman, this does not invalidate the seriousness of Shakespeare's purpose nor, within the restrictions imposed by his medium, the success of his execution. Henry is an appointed symbol of majesty, and the action of the play is directed with the most elaborate care to show him doing everything that the age expected of the perfect king.[5] If real life is not quite as simple as that, no matter. Human virtue is always muddied, or it would not be human; epic is the art that on special occasions transforms it into the ideal.

[5] See J. H. Walter, Arden edition, xvii-xviii. Thus Henry is the intimate of scholars and divines and seeks the advice of wise counsellors; he banishes idlers, parasites and flatterers, although he can unbend in the company of ordinary men; he is master of his passions and does not give way to lust or anger; he accepts all the cares of state, burdensome as they are, and recognises titles and ceremony at their true rate; he has the sinews to protect his kingdom, and, if necessary, to conduct a righteous war, but at the same time he knows that war has many evils and he acknowledges his duty to see that it is not waged without real cause; personally brave, he raises the spirits of his men; he rules mercifully but justly, being ready to sacrifice his friends if they threaten the public safety; he maintains order and the country is united under him.

PART THREE

Viewpoints

William Butler Yeats

The deeds of Coriolanus, Hamlet, Timon, Richard II had no obvious use, were, indeed, no more than the expression of their personalities, and so it was thought Shakespeare was accusing them, and telling us to be careful lest we deserve the like accusations. It did not occur to the critics that you cannot know a man from his actions because you cannot watch him in every kind of circumstance, and that men are made useless to the State as often by abundance as by emptiness, and that a man's business may at times be revelation, and not reformation. Fortinbras was, it is likely enough, a better king than Hamlet would have been, Aufidius was a more reasonable man than Coriolanus, Henry V was a better man-at-arms than Richard II, but, after all, were not those others who changed nothing for the better and many things for the worse greater in the Divine Hierarchies? Blake has said that 'the roaring of lions, the howling of wolves, the raging of the stormy sea, and the destructive sword are portions of Eternity, too great for the eye of man,' but Blake belonged by right to the ages of Faith, and thought the State of less moment than the Divine Hierarchies. Because reason can only discover completely the use of those obvious actions which everybody admires, and because every character was to be judged by efficiency in action, Shakespearian criticism became a vulgar worshipper of success. I have turned over many books in the library at Stratford-on-Avon, and I have found in nearly all an antithesis, which grew in clearness and violence as the century grew older, between two types, whose representatives were Richard II, 'sentimental,' 'weak,' 'selfish,' 'insincere,' and Henry V, 'Shakespeare's only hero.' These books took the same delight in abasing

"At Stratford-on-Avon," by W. B. Yeats. From Essays and Introductions *(New York: The Macmillan Company, 1961; London: Macmillan and Company, Ltd., 1961). The essay first appeared in 1901.*

Richard II that schoolboys do in persecuting some boy of fine temperament, who has weak muscles and a distaste for school games. And they had the admiration for Henry V that schoolboys have for the sailor or soldier hero of a romance in some boys' paper. I cannot claim any minute knowledge of these books, but I think that these emotions began among the German critics, who perhaps saw something French and Latin in Richard II, and I know that Professor Dowden, whose book I once read carefully, first made these emotions eloquent and plausible. He lived in Ireland, where everything has failed, and he meditated frequently upon the perfection of character which had, he thought, made England successful, for, as we say, 'cows beyond the water have long horns.' He forgot that England, as Gordon has said, was made by her adventurers, by her people of wildness and imagination and eccentricity; and thought that Henry V, who only seemed to be these things because he had some commonplace vices, was not only the typical Anglo-Saxon, but the model Shakespeare held up before England; and he even thought it worth while pointing out that Shakespeare himself was making a large fortune while he was writing about Henry's victories. In Professor Dowden's successors this apotheosis went further; and it reached its height at a moment of imperialistic enthusiasm, of ever-deepening conviction that the commonplace shall inherit the earth, when somebody of reputation, whose name I cannot remember, wrote that Shakespeare admired this one character alone out of all his characters. The Accusation of Sin produced its necessary fruit, hatred of all that was abundant, extravagant, exuberant, of all that sets a sail for shipwreck, and flattery of the commonplace emotions and conventional ideals of the mob, the chief Paymaster of accusation.

I cannot believe that Shakespeare looked on his Richard II with any but sympathetic eyes, understanding indeed how ill-fitted he was to be king, at a certain moment of history, but understanding that he was lovable and full of capricious fancy, 'a wild creature' as Pater has called him. The man on whom Shakespeare modelled him had been full of French elegances as he knew from Holinshed, and had given life a new luxury, a new splendour, and been 'too friendly' to his friends, 'too favourable' to his enemies. And certainly Shakespeare had these things in his head when he made his king fail, a little because he lacked some qualities that were doubtless common among his scullions, but more because he had certain qualities that are uncommon in all ages. To suppose that Shakespeare preferred the men who deposed his king is to suppose that Shakespeare judged men with the eyes of a Municipal Councillor weighing the merits of a Town Clerk; and that had he been by when Verlaine cried out from his bed, 'Sir, you have been made by the stroke of a pen, but I have been made by the breath of God,' he would have thought the Hospital Superintendent the better man. He saw indeed, as I think, in Richard II the defeat that awaits all, whether they be artist or saint, who find themselves where men ask of them a rough energy and have nothing to give but some contemplative virtue, whether lyrical fantasy, or sweetness of temper, or dreamy dignity, or love of God, or love of His creatures. He saw that such a man through sheer bewilderment and impatience can become as unjust or as violent as any common man, any Bolingbroke or Prince John, and yet remain 'that sweet lovely rose.' The courtly and saintly ideals of the Middle Ages were fading, and the practical ideals of the modern age had begun to threaten the unuseful dome of the sky; Merry England was fading, and yet it was not so faded that the poets could not watch the procession of the world with that untroubled sympathy for men as they are, as apart from all they do and seem, which is the substance of tragic irony.

Shakespeare cared little for the State, the source of all our judgments, apart from its shows and splendours, its turmoils and battles, its flamings-out of the uncivilised heart. He did indeed think it wrong to overturn a king, and thereby to swamp peace in civil war, and the historical plays from *Henry IV* to *Richard III,* that monstrous birth and last sign of the wrath of Heaven, are a fulfilment of the prophecy of the Bishop of Carlisle, who was 'raised up by God' to make it; but he had no nice sense of utilities, no ready balance to measure deeds, like that fine instrument, with all the latest improvements, Gervinus and Professor Dowden handle so skilfully. He meditated as Solomon, not as Bentham meditated, upon blind ambitions, untoward accidents, and capricious passions, and the world was almost as empty in his eyes as it must be in the eyes of God.

> Tired with all these, for restful death I cry;—
> As, to behold desert a beggar born,

And needy nothing trimm'd in jollity,
  And purest faith unhappily forsworn,
And gilded honour shamefully misplaced,
  And maiden virtue rudely strumpeted,
And right perfection wrongfully disgraced,
  And strength by limping sway disabled,
And art made tongue-tied by authority,
  And folly, doctor-like, controlling skill,
And simple truth miscall'd simplicity,
  And captive good attending captain ill:
Tired with all these, from these would I be gone,
Save that, to die, I leave my love alone.

The Greeks, a certain scholar has told me, considered that myths are the activities of the Daimons, and that the Daimons shape our characters and our lives. I have often had the fancy that there is some one myth for every man, which, if we but knew it, would make us understand all he did and thought. Shakespeare's myth, it may be, describes a wise man who was blind from very wisdom, and an empty man who thrust him from his place, and saw all that could be seen from very emptiness. It is in the story of Hamlet, who saw too great issues everywhere to play the trivial game of life, and of Fortinbras, who came from fighting battles about 'a little patch of ground' so poor that one of his captains would not give 'six ducats' to 'farm it,' and who was yet acclaimed by Hamlet and by all as the only befitting king. And it is in the story of Richard II, that unripened Hamlet, and of Henry V, that ripened Fortinbras. To pose character against character was an element in Shakespeare's art, and scarcely a play is lacking in characters that are the complement of one another, and so, having made the vessel of porcelain, Richard II, he had to make the vessel of clay, Henry V. He makes him the reverse of all that Richard was. He has the gross vices, the coarse nerves, of one who is to rule among violent people, and he is so little 'too friendly' to his friends that he bundles them out of doors when their time is over. He is as remorseless and undistinguished as some natural force, and the finest thing in his play is the way his old companions fall out of it broken-hearted or on their way to the gallows; and instead of that lyricism which rose out of Richard's mind like the jet of a fountain to fall again where it had risen, instead of that fantasy too enfolded in its own sincerity to make any thought the hour had need of, Shakespeare has given him a resounding rhetoric that moves men as a leading article does to-day. His purposes are so intelligible to everybody that everybody talks of him as if he succeeded, although he fails in the end, as all men great and little fail in Shakespeare. His conquests abroad are made nothing by a woman turned warrior. That boy he and Katharine were to 'compound,' 'half French, half English,' 'that' was to 'go to Constantinople and take the Turk by the beard,' turns out a saint and loses all his father had built up at home and his own life.

Shakespeare watched Henry V not indeed as he watched the greater souls in the visionary procession, but cheerfully, as one watches some handsome spirited horse, and he spoke his tale, as he spoke all tales, with tragic irony.

A. C. Bradley

. . . To come, then, to Henry. Both as prince and as king he is deservedly a favourite, and particularly so with English readers, being, as he is, perhaps the most distinctively English of all Shakespeare's men. In *Henry V.* he is treated as a national hero. In this play he has lost much of the wit which in him seems to have depended on contact with Falstaff, but he has also laid aside the most serious faults of his youth. He inspires in a high degree fear, enthusiasm, and affection; thanks to his beautiful modesty he has the charm which is lacking to another mighty warrior, Coriolanus; his youthful escapades have given him an understanding of simple folk, and sympathy with them; he is the author of the saying, 'There is some soul of goodness in things evil'; and he is much more obviously religious than most of Shakespeare's heroes. Having these and other fine qualities, and being without certain dangerous tendencies which mark the tragic heroes, he is, perhaps, the most *efficient* character drawn by Shakespeare, unless

"The Rejection of Falstaff," by A. C. Bradley. From Oxford Lectures on Poetry, *2nd ed. (London: Macmillan & Co., Ltd., 1909).*

Ulysses, in *Troilus and Cressida,* is his equal. And so he has been described as Shakespeare's ideal man of action; nay, it has even been declared that here for once Shakespeare plainly disclosed his own ethical creed, and showed us his ideal, not simply of a man of action, but of a man.

But Henry is neither of these. The poet who drew Hamlet and Othello can never have thought that even the ideal man of action would lack that light upon the brow which at once transfigures them and marks their doom. It is as easy to believe that, because the lunatic, the lover, and the poet are not far apart, Shakespeare would have chosen never to have loved and sung. Even poor Timon, the most inefficient of the tragic heroes, has something in him that Henry never shows. Nor is it merely that his nature is limited: if we follow Shakespeare and look closely at Henry, we shall discover with the many fine traits a few less pleasing. Henry IV. describes him as the noble image of his own youth; and, for all his superiority to his father, he is still his father's son, the son of the man whom Hotspur called a 'vile politician.' Henry's religion, for example, is genuine, it is rooted in his modesty; but it is also superstitious—an attempt to buy off supernatural vengeance for Richard's blood; and it is also in part political, like his father's projected crusade. Just as he went to war chiefly because, as his father told him, it was the way to keep factious nobles quiet and unite the nation, so when he adjures the Archbishop to satisfy him as to his right to the French throne, he knows very well that the Archbishop *wants* the war, because it will defer and perhaps prevent what he considers the spoliation of the Church. This same strain of policy is what Shakespeare marks in the first soliloquy in *Henry IV.*, where the prince describes his riotous life as a mere scheme to win him glory later. It implies that readiness to use other people as means to his own ends which is a conspicuous feature in his father; and it reminds us of his father's plan of keeping himself out of the people's sight while Richard was making himself cheap by his incessant public appearances. And if I am not mistaken there is a further likeness. Henry is kindly and pleasant to every one as Prince, to every one deserving as King; and he is so not merely out of policy: but there is no sign in him of a strong affection for any one, such an affection as we recognise at a glance in Hamlet and Horatio, Brutus and Cassius, and many more. We do not find this in *Henry V.*, not even in the noble address to Lord Scroop, and in *Henry IV.* we find, I think, a liking for Falstaff and Poins, but no more: there is no more than a liking, for instance, in his soliloquy over the supposed corpse of his fat friend, and he never speaks of Falstaff to Poins with any affection. The truth is, that the members of the family of Henry IV. have love for one another, but they cannot spare love for any one outside their family, which stands firmly united, defending its royal position against attack and instinctively isolating itself from outside influence.

Thus I would suggest that Henry's conduct in his rejection of Falstaff is in perfect keeping with his character on its unpleasant side as well as on its finer; and that, so far as Henry is concerned, we ought not to feel surprise at it. And on this view we may even explain the strange incident of the Chief Justice being sent back to order Falstaff to prison (for there is no sign of any such uncertainty in the text as might suggest an interpolation by the players). Remembering his father's words about Henry, 'Being incensed, he's flint,' and remembering in *Henry V.* his ruthlessness about killing the prisoners when he is incensed, we may imagine that, after he had left Falstaff and was no longer influenced by the face of his old companion, he gave way to anger at the indecent familiarity which had provoked a compromising scene on the most ceremonial of occasions and in the presence alike of court and crowd, and that he sent the Chief Justice back to take vengeance. And this is consistent with the fact that in the next play we find Falstaff shortly afterwards not only freed from prison, but unmolested in his old haunt in Eastcheap, well within ten miles of Henry's person. His anger had soon passed, and he knew that the requisite effect had been produced both on Falstaff and on the world.

But all this, however true, will not solve our problem. It seems, on the contrary, to increase its difficulty. For the natural conclusion is that Shakespeare *intended* us to feel resentment against Henry. And yet that cannot be, for it implies that he meant the play to end disagreeably; and no one who understands Shakespeare at all will consider that supposition for a moment credible. No; he must have meant the play to end pleasantly, although he made Henry's action consistent. And hence it follows that he must have intended our sympathy with Falstaff to be so far weakened when the rejection-scene arrives that his discomfiture should be satisfactory to us; that we should enjoy this sudden reverse of enormous hopes (a thing always ludicrous if sympathy is absent); that we should approve the moral judgment that falls on him; and so should pass lightly over that disclosure of unpleasant traits in the King's character which Shakespeare was too true an artist to suppress. Thus our pain and resentment, if we feel them, are wrong, in the sense that they do not answer to the dramatist's intention. But it does not follow that they are wrong in a further sense. They may be right, because the dramatist has missed what he aimed at. And this, though the dramatist was Shakespeare, is what I would suggest. In the Falstaff scenes he overshot his mark. He created so extraordinary a being, and fixed him so firmly on his intellectual throne, that when he sought to dethrone him he could not. The moment comes when we are to look at Falstaff in a serious light, and the comic hero is to figure as a baffled schemer; but we cannot make the required change, either in our attitude or in our sympathies. We wish Henry a glorious reign and much joy of his crew of hypocritical politicians, lay and clerical; but our hearts go with Falstaff to the Fleet, or, if necessary, to Arthur's bosom or wheresomever he is.[1]

Elmer Edgar Stoll

. . . Some readers may object a little to Henry's obtrusive morality and his familiarity with the Most High. They may be reminded of later czars and kaisers, likewise engaged in wars of aggression, and be inclined to call it all hypocrisy or official cant. Shakespeare surely did not mean it so; the Elizabethans would not have taken it so; and such monarchs, again, like their parties, are specimens of times and manners, now long out of date, but not out of date in the age of Elizabeth. In any case, Shakespeare has deliberately brushed away much of the piety clinging to him in Holinshed. He has added, to be sure, the prayer the night before the battle, in which he speaks of King

[1] That from the beginning Shakespeare intended Henry's accession to be Falstaff's catastrophe is clear from the fact that, when the two characters first appear, Falstaff is made to betray at once the hopes with which he looks foward to Henry's reign. See the First Part of *Henry IV*, Act I, Scene ii.

Richard's death. But that really is a relief; Henry is not so pious as penitent, and would make amends for his father's wrong, by which he profits. And a striking positive change is made when the action is about to begin. The speech he now utters (IV, iii, 18-67) . . . is all of honor; but the corresponding passage in Holinshed has something of the twang and snuffle of a Puritan preacher's cant:

> But if we should fight in trust of multitude of men, and so get the victorie (our minds being prone to pride), we should thereupon peradventure ascribe the victorie not so much to the gift of God, as to our owne puissance, and thereby provoke his high indignation and displeasure against us.

That, for a man of action, at such a moment, is not in Shakespeare's vein. Piety and humility for the night-time; but "amid the clang of arms," as Mr. Stone says, he would have his hero "speak in a rapture of martial ardor which sweeps every other thought from his mind." Now he must think only of battle and drink delight of battle. Instead of preaching in such an hour or praying, Shakespeare would have him assert himself, let himself go a bit, like, say, George Washington, another hero who sometimes seemed something of a prig and (in popular legend at least) was always the pink of propriety, but who in battle went so far as to break out spontaneously into oaths. "God's will!" cries King Henry, "I pray thee, wish not one man more . . . God's peace! I would not lose so great an honour." Like Nelson at Copenhagen, he "would not be elsewhere for thousands." Like Roland of old, he would not have wound his horn. "The game's afoot," as he cried to his men before Harfleur; his blood is up; and the name of God rises to his lips only in oaths or in the war-cry, "God for Harry, England, and St. George." Like every man of action, when the time of action arrives he thinks of nothing—feels the need of nothing—save to get into it. And in that hour he has no religion but that of the old English adage, "God helps him who helps himself."

Was Henry, then, as some have thought, Shakespeare's ideal? Gervinus and other German critics have declared he was, being the antithesis of Richard II and Hamlet. Some of them have even gone so far as to say that Henry is Shakespeare himself, with his practical genius and well-balanced nature, his taste for the low as well as the lofty, and his sense of humor in the midst of duty—his liking for play when at work. Mr. W. B. Yeats holds just the contrary. Poet of the Celtic twilight, of them that went forth to battle but always fell, he thinks that Shakespeare infinitely preferred Richard; and that Henry is given the "gross vices and coarse nerves," and "the resounding rhetoric, as of a leading article," which befit a man who succeeds, though his success was really failure. "Shakespeare watched Henry V, not indeed as he watched the greater souls in the visionary procession, but cheerfully, as one watches some handsome spirited horse, and he spoke his tale, as he spoke all tales, with tragic irony." But when Shakespeare—when any popular dramatist—is ironical, we the people must needs know it; or else his popular art has failed him and missed the mark. Here is no evidence of either. Instead of being sly, or insinuating, or pregnant of innuendo, he is more exuberant and enthusiastic than usual; the choruses, which are the authentic voice of the poet himself, put that beyond the peradventure of a doubt. And the likelihood is that Professor Dowden is nearer the truth; Henry V, at least in some measure, approaches Shakespeare's ideal of the practical man, which is not his highest ideal. Shakespeare, no doubt, admired success, though without worshipping it; he himself succeeded, not inconsiderably in his brief two score and ten; but the men he admired most, I daresay, were the finer spirits such as Hamlet, Brutus, or Prospero, whether they succeeded or failed. It was their devotion and gallantry that he admired, not (pessimistically or sentimentally) their devotion and gallantry foiled or thrown away.

It is more to the point to say that Henry is the ideal of England, not Shakespeare's but his country's notion of their hero-king. He is the king that audiences at the Globe would have him be. This is particularly true as regards what we nowadays consider his bragging, his priggishness and cant. The obtrusive morality and piety were expected; for that matter they are like the sort of thing you find in a Speech from the Throne or our American Presidential Thanksgiving proclamations at the present day. Officially, piety has been ever in favor; even in ungodly America ceremonies so diverse as the laying of a corner stone and the conferring of the German degree of Ph.D. are performed in the name of the Father, the Son, and the Holy Ghost; and in the new Assembly of Southern Ireland, I notice, the order is given by the Speaker to "call the roll in the name of God."

And on the Elizabethan stage piety and morality are as inseparable from the ideal king as the crown on his head, the royal "we" in his mouth, or the "strut" (lingering down to the eighteenth century to be admired by Sir Roger de Coverley) with which his royal legs must tread the stage. There is in all Elizabethan dramatic art something naïve—something self-descriptive—in the lines, which in the three centuries of evolution towards the more purely and strictly dramatic has nearly disappeared. The wicked, like Richard III in his first soliloquy, know that they are wicked; the good, that they are good; heroes like Julius Caesar boast and vaunt their prowess; and a king, like a god on the stage, must every minute remember, and make us remember too, that he is nothing less. Henry's preaching, swaggering, and swinging of the scepter may repel us a bit today; but that is because as we read we democratically take him for no more than a man, as people at the Globe did not nor were expected to do. Even we, at the theater, are perhaps not so different and enlightened as we think. King Edward VII, not emulating the ceremoniousness of his ancestors, walked and talked like other people; but on the stage, not more than a score of years ago, Richard Mansfield, as Henry V, found it expedient to strut and swagger a bit again, in the fashion that pleased Sir Roger.

Caroline F. E. Spurgeon

. . . I see no running imagery in the first or second part of *Henry IV*. In *Henry V*, however, the opening words of the chorus—sighing for 'a Muse of fire' to 'ascend the brightest heaven of invention'—seem to give the key-note to the dominating atmosphere of the earlier and best part of the play, swift and soaring movement; and it is not mere chance, I think, that we find, through the play, an unusual number of images of the flight of birds, which for our forefathers symbolised the swiftest movement known to man.

The desire adequately to convey to the audience this particular combination of intense swiftness and dignity, with the consciousness of the limitations of the rude and primitive theatre, dominates the opening prologue. Indeed, the urgent appeal to the onlookers to use their

"Flight Images in Henry V," *by Caroline F. E. Spurgeon. From* Shakespeare's Imagery And What It Tells Us *(Cambridge: Cambridge University Press, 1935).*

imaginations and piece out with their thoughts the imperfections of actors and stage, is the main theme of the vivid and stirring poetry of all five prologues.

The brilliant description of the fleet on its way from Southampton to Harfleur opens,

> Thus with imagined wing our swift scene flies
> In motion of no less celerity
> Than that of thought.

Later when, on the return journey, the king is crossing from Calais to Dover, the audience are urged to use their thoughts with the strength or swiftness of a bird's flight, to

> Heave him away upon your winged thoughts
> Athwart the sea.

Henry himself, when making ready for France, with all the expedition possible, falls into the same simile:

> let our proportions for these wars
> Be soon collected, and all things thought upon
> That may with reasonable swiftness add
> More feathers to our wings.

He measures emotion—its height and depth—by the same picture of the flight of a bird; though the king's affections, he tells his soldiers, are 'higher mounted' than those of common folk, 'yet, when they stoop, they stoop with the like wing'; and when arguing later with them as to the king's responsibility for the fate of individuals in battle, he points out that those of his soldiers who have previously been evil-doers—thieves or murderers—meet their deserts in war, though they may have 'defeated the law and outrun native punishment, though they can outstrip men, they have no wings to fly from God: war is His beadle, war is His vengeance'.

Finally, the Duke of York's moving cry, when he finds his friend dead on the battle field, sums up, in the last two words, with Shakespeare's characteristic magic, the whole force of this favourite image:

> Tarry, dear cousin Suffolk!
> My soul shall thine keep company to heaven;
> Tarry, sweet soul, for mine, then fly abreast.

We may note, that, though birds are not mentioned in any one of these images, yet the picture of their sure and soaring flight, swift and strong, is in each intense and vivid.

The little scene of the Dauphin with his spirited horse (3. 7) adds to this feeling of strong and soaring motion, and coming where it does, just before the description of the 'poor condemned English', sitting by their camp-fires, patient and sad, lean and pale as ghosts, it points the contrast vividly between them and the 'over-lusty' French. The Dauphin's horse bounds from the earth like a tennis ball ('as if his entrails were hairs'), he is 'le cheval volant, the Pegasus', 'he trots the air', 'the earth sings when he touches it', 'he is pure air and fire', and 'when I bestride him', declares his master proudly, 'I soar, I am a hawk'. And the next minute we are with 'Harry in the night', 'walking from watch to watch, from tent to tent', cheering his war-worn soldiers.

Mark Van Doren

. . . "Henry V" has its splendors and its secondary attractions, but the forces in it are not unified. The reason probably is that for Shakespeare they had ceased to be genuine forces. He marshals for his task a host of substitute powers, but the effect is often hollow. The style strains itself to bursting, the hero is stretched until he struts on tiptoe and is still strutting at the last insignificant exit, and war is emptied of its tragic content. The form of the historical drama had been the tragic form; its dress is borrowed here, but only borrowed. The heroic idea splinters into a thousand starry fragments, fine as fragments but lighted from no single source.

Everywhere efforts are made to be striking, and they succeed. But the success is local. "Henry V" does not succeed as a whole because its author lacks adequate dramatic matter; or because, veering so suddenly away from tragedy, he is unable to free himself from the accidents of its form; or because, with "Julius Caesar" and "Hamlet" on his horizon, he finds himself less interested than before in heroes who are men of action and yet is not at the moment provided with a dramatic language for saying so. Whatever the cause, we discover that we are being entertained from the top of his mind. There is much there to glitter and please us, but what pleases us has less body than what once did so and soon will do so with still greater abundance again.

The prologues are the first sign of Shakespeare's imperfect dramatic faith. Their verse is wonderful but it has to be, for it is doing the work which the play ought to be doing, it is a substitute for scene and action. "O for a Muse of fire," the poet's apology begins. The prologues are everywhere apologetic; they are saying that no stage, this one or any other, is big enough or wealthy enough to present the "huge and proper life" of Henry's wars; this cockpit cannot hold the vasty fields of France, there will be no veritable horses in any scene, the ship-boys on the masts and the camp-fires at Agincourt will simply have to be imagined. Which it is the business of the play to make them be, as Shakespeare has known and will know again. The author of "Romeo and Juliet" had not been sorry because his stage was a piece of London rather than the whole of Verona, and the storm in "King Lear" will begin without benefit of description.

. . . The second sign of genius at loose ends is a radical and indeed an astounding inflation in the style. Passages of boasting and exhortation are in place, but even the best of them, whether from the French or from the English side, have a forced, shrill, windy sound, as if their author were pumping his muse for dear life in the hope that mere speed and plangency might take the place of matter. For a few lines like

> Familiar in his mouth as household words (IV, iii, 52)
>
> The singing masons building roofs of gold (I, ii, 198)
>
> I see you stand like greyhounds in the slips,
> Straining upon the start (III, i, 31-2)

there are hundreds like

> The native mightiness and fate of him (II, iv, 64)
>
> With ample and brim fullness of his force (I, ii, 150)
>
> That caves and womby vaultages of France
> Shall chide your trespass and return your mock.
> (II, iv, 124-5)

Mightiness and fate, ample and brim, caves and vaultages, trespass and mock—such couplings attest the poet's desperation, the rhetorician's extremity. They spring up everywhere, like birds from undergrowth: sweet and honey'd, open haunts and popularity, thrive and ripen, crown and seat, right and title, right and conscience, kings and monarchs, means and might, aim and butt, large and ample, taken and impounded, frank and uncurbed, success and conquest, desert and merit, weight and worthiness, duty and zeal, savage and inhuman, botch and bungle, garnish'd and deck'd, assembled and collected, sinister and awkward, culled and choice-drawn, o'er-hang and jutty, waste and desolation, cool and temperate, flexure and low bending, signal and ostent, vainness and self-glorious pride. Shakespeare has perpetrated them before, as when in "Henry VI" he coupled ominous and fearful, trouble and disturb, substance and authority, and absurd and reasonless. But never has he perpetrated them with such thoughtless frequency. Nor has he at this point developed the compound epithet into that interesting mannerism—the only mannerism he ever submitted to—which is to be so noticeable in his next half-dozen plays, including "Hamlet."

The third sign is a direct and puerile appeal to the patriotism of the audience, a dependence upon sentiments outside the play that can be counted on, once they are tapped, to pour in and repair the deficiencies of the action. Unable to achieve a dramatic unity out of the materials before him, Shakespeare must grow lyrical about the unity of England; politics must substitute for poetry. He cannot take England for granted as the scene of conflicts whose greatness will imply its greatness. It must be great itself, and the play says so—unconvincingly. There are no conflicts. The traitors Scroop, Cambridge, and Grey are happy to lose their heads for England (II, ii), and the battles in France, even though the enemy's host is huge and starvation takes its toll, are bound to be won by such fine English fellows as we have here. If the French have boasted beforehand, the irony of their doing so was obvious from the start. But it was patriotism, shared as a secret between the author and his audience, that made it obvious. It was not drama.

And a fourth sign is the note of gaiety that takes the place here of high passion. The treasure sent to Henry by the Dauphin is discovered at the end of the first act to be tennis-balls: an insult which the young king returns in a speech about matching rackets and playing sets—his idiom for bloody war. When the treachery of Scroop, Cambridge, and Grey is detected on the eve of his departure for France he stages their discomfiture somewhat as games are undertaken, and with a certain sporting relish watches their faces as they read their dooms. The conversation of the French leaders as they wait for the sun to rise on Agincourt is nervous as thoroughbreds are nervous, or champion athletes impatient for a tournament to commence; their camp is a locker room, littered with attitudes no less than uniforms (III, vii). The deaths of York and Suffolk the next day are images of how young knights should die. They kiss each other's gashes, wearing their red blood like roses in the field, and spending their last breath in terms so fine that Exeter, reporting to the King, is overcome by "the pretty and sweet manner of it" (IV, vi, 28). And of course there are the scenes where Katharine makes fritters of English, waiting to be wooed (III, iv) and wooed at last (V, ii) by Henry Plantagenet, "king of good fellows." "The truth is," said Dr. Johnson, "that the poet's matter failed him in the fifth act, and he was glad to fill it up with whatever he could get; and not even Shakespeare can write well without a proper subject. It is a vain endeavour for the most skilful hand to cultivate barrenness, or to paint upon vacuity." That is harsh, but its essence cannot be ignored. The high spirits in which the scenes are written have their attraction, but they are no substitute for intensity.

. . . Shakespeare has forgotten the glittering young god whom Vernon described in "Henry IV"—plumed like an estridge or like an eagle lately bathed, shining like an image in his golden coat, as full of spirit as the month of May, wanton as a youthful goat, a feathered Mercury, an angel dropped down from the clouds. The figure whom he has groomed to be the ideal English king, all plumes and smiles and decorated courage, collapses here into a mere good fellow, a hearty undergraduate with enormous initials on his chest. The reason must be that Shakespeare has little interest in the ideal English king. He has done what rhetoric could do to give us a young heart whole in honor, but his imagination has already sped forward to Brutus and Hamlet: to a kind of hero who is no less honorable than Henry but who will tread on thorns as he takes the path of duty—itself unclear, and crossed by other paths of no man's making. Henry is Shakespeare's last attempt at the great man who is also simple. Henceforth he will show greatness as either perplexing or perplexed; and Hamlet will be both. . . .

J. Dover Wilson

Every reader of Hazlitt has now come to make allowances for what Professor Elton calls 'the astonishing gusts of political fury' that 'sweep over his pages amidst the most innocent literary criticism.' One such bitter gust . . . may be encountered at the opening of the essay on *Henry V* in his *Characters of Shakespeare's Plays.* All is calm and bright in the previous section. 'The characters of Hotspur and Prince Henry are two of the most beautiful and dramatic . . . that were ever drawn'; and though Hotspur is preferred to Hal on the ground 'that we never could forgive the Prince's treatment of Falstaff': the reflection is rather playful than seriously intended. Turn the page, however, and we are met with a hail-storm of abuse, directed at the devoted head of Henry V, but embracing also his conduct as Prince of Wales. He is 'fond of war and low company—we know little else of him'; he is 'careless, dissolute, and ambitious—idle or doing mischief'; in private he had 'no idea of the common decencies of life'; in public affairs he has 'no idea of any rule of right or wrong but brute force'—and so on for a paragraph of considerable length, until, all passion spent, Hazlitt as suddenly and almost apologetically returns to business as a critic, with 'So much for the politics of this play, now for the poetry'. It is easy to see what happened. Shakespeare's *Henry V* stands for everything that Hazlitt most hated in politics: absolute monarchy, the feudal system, the military virtues, the conquest of his beloved France, above all, perhaps, the conservative Englishman. The realization of this swept over him upon reading the play, especially as he read the speeches of the Archbishop of Canterbury at the beginning of it, and carried him off his feet. Yet his paragraph, no less

"Introduction: Back to Johnson," by J. Dover Wilson. From The Fortunes of Falstaff *(Cambridge: Cambridge University Press, 1943).*

an immediate product of French revolutionary ideas and hatred for the Holy Alliance than Shelley's almost contemporaneous *Prometheus Unbound,* is the origin of all later aesthetic criticism of Prince Hal. Reinforced by the reigning pacifism of the early twentieth century, it inspired an extraordinary outburst in a widely read book on Shakespeare by Mr. Masefield in 1911, still quoted with approval in some quarters. Most important of all, it was adopted a little earlier, in a more temperate and therefore more persuasive form, by Andrew Bradley, made use of to explain Falstaff's dismissal, and thus became one of the foundations of his critical edifice.

Shakespeare lived in the world of Plato and St. Augustine; since the French Revolution we have been living in the world of Rousseau; and this fact lays many traps of misunderstanding for unsuspecting readers, of which the foregoing is a particular instance. And of all the plays, those dealing with historical or political themes are most liable to be thus misread. But Dr. Johnson still lived in Shakespeare's world, a world which was held together, and could only be held together, by authority based on and working through a carefully preserved gradation of rank. . . .

> The prince [he writes] who is the hero both of the comick and tragick part, is a young man of great abilities and violent passions, whose sentiments are right, though his actions are wrong; whose virtues are obscured by negligence, and whose understanding is dissipated by levity. In his idle hours he is rather loose than wicked, and when the occasion forces out his latent qualities, he is great without effort, and brave without tumult. The trifler is roused into a hero, and the hero again reposes in the trifler. The character is great, original, and just.

Perusing the play 'without ambition of critical discoveries', he clearly accepted the story at its face value: as a dramatic account of the unregenerate youth of one of the greatest English kings. The idea of looking below the surface never presented itself to him. Above all he thought of Hal as a prince, that is, as a being differing not only in rank but almost in kind from other men. Such ideas may be, or may have seemed to the nineteenth century, old-fashioned, but they are not primitive. There was nothing primitive in the mind of the President of the Literary Club.

Paul Jorgensen

In his portrait of Henry V as general, Shakespeare demonstrated that whatever deficiencies the play might have in representing army life were not due to lack of pains. In no other military portrait—Falstaff not excepted—can we say with more assurance that here the dramatist made a careful study of military theory, and sketched character with the theory constantly in mind. Not even Holinshed was more closely studied for this purpose. In fact, although from Holinshed (and partially from *The Famous Victories of Henry the Fifth*) came the outline of Henry V as a religious, efficient warrior, Shakespeare derived most of Henry's conduct and speech as a general from the precepts of military books.

The indebtedness which resulted was different not merely in degree from that of his other military portraits; it was different in kind. For the first time, Shakespeare risked the consequences of drawing a handbook-perfect officer. In all of his other portraits he selected types or ranks interesting for wayward traits, either of contentiousness or of fraudulent practices. To attempt making his main dramatic figure not only "the mirror of all Christian kings" (V. Chorus.6) but the mirror of a Christian general, and to deprive him further of the dissensions available in a divided command, was to forfeit in advance most of the playwright's dependable stratagems for good drama. We shall, to be sure, find that Shakespeare discovered opportunities for a few instances of minor tension within this model portrait, but these are insufficient to make Henry one of Shakespeare's most interesting military studies.

Especial difficulty confronted Shakespeare in his plan to create Henry as a Christian conqueror. Marlowe made a luckier choice in his pagan Tamburlaine, for more interesting irregularities were thus possible: keeping captive emperors in cages, using them as horses for the conqueror's chariot, and making spectacular slaughter of virgins delegated to plead for mercy. All this was denied Shakespeare by the

"Military Rank," by Paul Jorgensen. From Shakespeare's Military World *(Berkeley: University of California Press, 1956).*

handbooks which he conscientiously followed. According to Sutcliffe;[1] for example, the Christian king as general is distinguished from the heathen Turk by his mercy toward opponents. And Henry V assures his enemy, "We are no tyrant, but a Christian king" (I. ii. 241). More specifically, Paul Ive's translation of Fourquevaux's *Instructions for the Warres* (1589) demands of the general: "If so be that he should have to do with a strong and puissant towne, I would never be of opinion he should use any force, if he might have it lovinglie and by honest composition."[2] Following this precept meant for Shakespeare softening an episode that in Holinshed had spectacular elements—the siege of Harfleur. In the historian's account, the city is sacked after a vigorous battle. Inducements of decorum might, of course, have deterred Shakespeare from presenting the full realities of such a spectacle, but a more immediate reason is evident in Henry's remark (III.vi. 118–120): "for when lenity and cruelty play for a kingdom, the gentler gamester is the soonest winner."

The same influence accounts for his emphasizing, instead of more exciting material rewards, a pious forbearance in victory. Henry's soldiers get no pillage or concubines like Tamburlaine's. Instead, the audience is treated to a rather somber episode involving the sentencing of Bardolph for stealing a pax from a church. The precept behind this austere substitution is typically expressed by Garrard: "Immediately upon the taking of the Towne, the prince or Generall . . . must enter into the Towne, with his sworde naked in his hand, and must goe to the principall Church to give God thanks for this victorie, and also to defend, that the ornaments which appertaine to the Church be not pulled down nor robbed. . . . Incontinently he must make cry through the Cittie, that none uppon payne of hanging neither take nor spoyle any Churches."[3]

If rejection of pillage was hard for the soldiers, refusal of personal glory in victory was the special austerity which Christian precepts demanded of the general. Henry is so solicitous in ascribing his victory to God, with no boasting or even close attention to the mechanics of triumph, that one wonders how Elizabethans, having tasted the richer

[1] Mathew Sutcliffe, *The Practice, Proceedings and Lawes of Armes* (1593), 12.
[2] Fourquevaux, *Warres,* 225.
[3] William Garrard, *The Arte of Warre* (1591), 304.

meat of Tamburlaine's boasting, reacted to Henry's piety. Possibly, having heard his stern command (IV.viii.118),

> Come, go we in procession to the village;
> And be it death proclaimed through our host
> To boast of this, or take that praise from God
> Which is his only,

many would innocently have asked, like Fluellen, "Is it not lawful, an please your Majesty, to tell how many is kill'd?" (IV.viii.121–122).

Elizabethans had, however, been well instructed in their own victories over Spain not to usurp any credit for themselves; and they would have recognized, though with suppressed regret, that Henry's conduct was praiseworthy. What is more, military literature of the age would have convinced them that his modesty was practical as well as model. In *An Arithmeticall Militare Treatise, named Stratioticos,* the work of Thomas and Leonard Digges, the general is advised to credit the victory first to God and secondly to his army, for by so doing he will "not only make his honourable Actions shine the more gloriouslie, but also wonderfully combine with harty good wyll his Souldiours to love and honor him." [4] The penalty for violating this code is even more tangible than the rewards for observing it. John Norden warned that if God finds generals attributing "their successe unto themselves, either in regard to their power, multitude, valour, policies or military stratagems, hee forthwith becommeth their enemie, and diminisheth their number, weakeneth their power, besotteth their devises, and maketh their policies of none effect." [5]

[4] Digges, *Stratioticos* (1579), sig. S1.
[5] John Norden, *The Mirror of Honor* (1597), 73.

Chronology of Important Dates

	Shakespeare	*Other Events*
1549		*The Booke of the Common Prayer.*
1564	William Shakespeare baptized at Stratford (April 26).	
1569		Beginning of the intermittent Anglo-Spanish war which is to last for nearly a generation.
1582	Married to Anne Hathaway.	
1587		Execution of Mary Stuart.
1588	Performance of the early comedies. (1588?-94)	Destruction of the Spanish Armada.
1590	Performance of the English histories. (1590?-99)	Rise of Essex. (1590-93)
1594	Shakespeare a sharer in the Lord Chamberlain's company.	
1595		Years of famine, disease, and natural disaster in England. The last years of Elizabeth see the end of her "compromise" system of rule. (1595-1600)
1597	Shakespeare's purchase of New Place, Stratford.	
1599	Opening of the Globe Theatre.	
1600	Performance of the great tragedies. (1600-1608?)	

	Shakespeare	*Other Events*
1601	Shakespeare's company hired to perform *Richard II.*	Rebellion of Essex.
1603		Death of Elizabeth I and accession of James I.
1604		The first parliament of James I: England informed of the new character of the monarchy.
1605		The Gunpowder Plot.
1605-17		Maladministration of England. Impending bankruptcy and court extravagance. Puritans alienated by the monarchy.
1608-13?	Performance of the last plays.	
1609	Publication of the *Sonnets.*	
1611		The King James translation of the Bible.
1616	Death of Shakespeare. (April 23)	Buckingham in favor. New tensions at court and increasing differences between social classes and religious persuasions.
1623	Publication of *First Folio.*	
1625		Death of James I and accession of Charles I.

Notes on the Editor and Contributors

RONALD BERMAN, the editor of this volume, teaches Renaissance literature at the University of California, San Diego. He is the author of a number of books and essays, among them *A Reader's Guide to Shakespeare's Plays.*

A. C. BRADLEY (1851-1935) was the most noted Shakespearean of the early twentieth century. His *Shakespearean Tragedy* was the high-water mark of character study as a critical mode.

GEOFFREY BULLOUGH is Professor of English Language and Literature, King's College, London. He is the editor of *Narrative and Dramatic Sources of Shakespeare.*

LILY B. CAMPBELL, Professor Emeritus of the University of California, Los Angeles, is the author of many studies of Renaissance literature. Her books include *Shakespeare's 'Histories': Mirrors of Elizabethan Policy* and *Shakespeare's Tragic Heroes: Slaves of Passion.*

UNA ELLIS-FERMOR (1894-1958) was best known as the author of *The Jacobean Drama* and *The Frontiers of Drama.* She was the general editor of the New Arden Shakespeare.

PAUL JORGENSEN is Professor of English literature at the University of California, Los Angeles. He is the author of numerous studies and bibliographies of Shakespeare.

M. M. REESE is the author of *The Tudors and Stuarts; Shakespeare: His World and His Work;* and *The Cease of Majesty.*

A. P. ROSSITER (1905-1957) was Lecturer at Durham and Cambridge. He wrote *English Drama* and *Angel With Horns.*

CAROLINE F. E. SPURGEON (1869-1941) was Professor of English literature at the University of London. She initiated the modern study of Shakespeare's language in *Shakespeare's Imagery And What It Tells Us.*

ELMER EDGAR STOLL was an iconoclastic American Shakespearean. His defenses of realism and attacks on less rigorous critics have been collected in *Art and Artifice in Shakespeare; Poets and Playwrights;* and *Shakespeare Studies.*

E. M. W. TILLYARD (1889-1962) was Master of Jesus College, Cambridge. He was best known for his work on the seventeenth century, exemplified by *The Elizabethan World Picture* and *The English Epic and its Background.*

DEREK TRAVERSI, who has held positions abroad in the British Council and British Institute, is the author of *An Approach to Shakespeare* and several other books on groups of Shakespeare's plays. He has been one of the critics associated with *Scrutiny.*

MARK VAN DOREN, Professor Emeritus at Columbia University, is a poet and literary critic.

CHARLES WILLIAMS (1886-1945) was a man of letters of singularly wide-ranging interests. His *Selected Writings* were edited by Anne Ridler in 1961.

J. DOVER WILSON, Professor at the University of Edinburgh, has been the most combative and fertile of modern Shakespeareans. His New Cambridge edition of the plays is well-known; among other works are *What Happens in Hamlet* and *The Fortunes of Falstaff.*

WILLIAM BUTLER YEATS (1865-1939), the greatest poet of modern times, needs no further identification.

Selected Bibliography

Berman, Ronald, *"Henry V," A Reader's Guide to Shakespeare's Plays*. Chicago: Scott, Foresman and Company, 1965. A detailed bibliography of scholarship and criticism.

Boughner, Daniel, "Pistol and the Roaring Boys," *Shakespeare Association Bulletin*, XI (1936), 226-37. An illuminating study of the lower depths of the Elizabethan world.

Goddard, H. C., *The Meaning of Shakespeare*. Chicago: Chicago University Press, 1951. Contains an account of the ironies which undercut the heroic tone of *Henry V*.

Granville-Barker, Harley, "From *Henry V* to *Hamlet*," *Studies in Shakespeare*, ed. Peter Alexander. London: Oxford University Press, 1964. This is a revised version of an essay which first appeared in 1925. It views *Henry V* as the culmination of Shakespeare's early style.

Hotson, Leslie, "Ancient Pistol," *Shakespeare's Sonnets Dated*. London: Rupert Hart-Davis, 1949. Valuable study of the chief minor character.

Palmer, John, *Political Characters of Shakespeare*. London: The Macmillan Company, 1945. Leisurely and sympathetic reading of the play.

Ribner, Irving, *The English History Play in the Age of Shakespeare*. Princeton: Princeton University Press, 1957. Useful for the background, but not very acute on the play itself.

Richmond, H. M., *Shakespeare's Political Plays*. New York: Random House, 1967. Argues acutely that Henry grows in maturity and stature in the course of the play.

Traversi, Derek, *Shakespeare from Richard II to Henry V*. London: Hollis and Carter, 1958. Best on *Richard II* and the Henry IV plays, but states clearly the limitations of Henry V and the "tragic" overtones of his experience.

Walter, J. H., ed., *King Henry V*. London: Methuen and Company, 1954. This volume of the New Arden series has a good introduction and is lavishly supplied with notes.

Wilson, J. Dover, ed., *Henry V*. Cambridge: Cambridge University Press, 1947. A useful critical essay and notes.

———, and T. C. Worsley, *Shakespeare's Histories at Stratford, 1951*. New York: Theatre Arts Books, 1952. Discusses the staging of the second tetralogy. Should be used in conjunction with the stage history in Dover Wilson's New Cambridge edition, xlviii-lvi.

DATE			
FEB 7 '80			
MAR 26 '87			